P9-BJW-635

MINUTE
GUIDE TO
OS/2® Warp

Jennifer Fulton

A Division of Macmillan Computer Publishing
A Prentice Hall Macmillan Company
201 West 103rd Street, Indianapolis, Indiana 46290 USA

To my friend Rhonda, who forgives me even when I don't call or write for months on end because she knows I'm an author with a deadline.

International Standard Book Number:1-56761-650-X

Library of Congress Catalog Card Number: 95-79782

97 96 95   8 7 6 5 4 3 2 1

Interpretation of the printing code: the rightmost number of the first series of numbers is the year of the book's printing; the rightmost number of the second series of numbers is the number of the book's printing. For example, a printing code of 95-1 shows that the first printing of the book occurred in 1995.

Printed in the United States of America

Publisher: Roland Elgey
Vice President and Publisher: Marie Butler-Knight
Editorial Services Director: Elizabeth Keaffaber
Publishing Manager: Barry Pruett
Product Development Manager: Faithe Wempen
Managing Editor: Michael Cunningham
Production Editor: Mark Enochs
Copy Editor: Audra Gable
Cover Designer: Dan Armstrong
Designer: Barbara Kordesh
Indexer: Brad Herriman
Team Supervisor: Brad Chinn
Production: Gary Adair, Angela Calvert, Dan Caparo, Kim Cofer, Dave Eason, Jennifer Eberhardt, Rob Falco, David Garratt, Joe Millay, Erika Millen, Beth Rago, Karen Walsh, Robert Wolf

Special thanks to C. Herbert Feltner for ensuring the technical accuracy of this book.

Contents

Introduction

"I just don't have enough time."

This is a common complaint whose solution lies not in finding more time (a day contains only 24 hours, after all), but in using time more wisely. That's where OS/2 Warp and this *10 Minute Guide* come into play. You see, OS/2 Warp saves you time because it enables you to interact with your computer in the most efficient manner. And this book gets you up and running with Warp in no time, with short easy lessons that fit into anyone's busy schedule.

What Exactly Is OS/2 Warp?

OS/2 Warp is an operating system (like DOS) that controls the actions of your computer. It's also a *graphical user interface* or GUI (like Windows) in which you select visual cues to indicate what you want the computer to do (instead of typing vague commands, as you do in DOS). Unlike Windows, however, you don't have to buy DOS to make OS/2 work because OS/2 is an operating system and a graphical user interface combined. Here are some of the ways OS/2 Warp makes your computer easier to use:

- You can work with more than one program at a time. For example, you could start a word processor and a spreadsheet program and switch between them at will.

- Warp's interface is easy to figure out and remember. That makes learning to use OS/2 simple and fun.

- All the programs that come with Warp have a similar look and feel. Once you learn how to use one program, you're well on your way to learning them all.

- Warp provides the tools you need to work. Its BonusPak includes a word processor, spreadsheet, chart maker, database, report writer, and more. You also get a full range of tools for your "toys," such as a sound card, fax modem, video capture board, and so on.

- OS/2 Warp makes it easy to get connected to the Internet. You can connect to the popular online service CompuServe with CIM for OS/2. In addition, HyperACCESS Lite makes it easy to connect to other online services, a BBS, or another PC.

How Is Warp Different from Windows?

As I said before, Warp is a combination operating system and graphical user interface, while Windows is only a GUI that needs DOS to run. If you already know how to use Windows, you'll find a lot of similarities in the way Warp works. But keep these differences in mind:

- Windows contains a separate File Manager and Program Manager; in Warp, you manage your files and programs from the same desktop.

- Windows uses icons to represent things such as files and programs. In Warp, these are called *objects*.

- If you have Windows, you can start it with Warp. You can even run your Windows programs from the Warp desktop without starting Windows at all!

- Windows organizes your programs into windows called program groups. In Warp, these are called *folders*, and they can contain not only program icons, but data-file icons as well. This enables you to organize your work by keeping similar programs and files together on your screen.

- When you want to move objects in Windows, you just click with the left mouse button and drag; in Warp, you use the *right* mouse button instead. You only use the left button to select an object.

- When you minimize a window in Windows, it shrinks to an icon at the bottom of your screen. In Warp, the window is removed from the screen entirely, giving you more space in which to work. To reactivate the window, you switch to it by select ing it from the Window List (similar to the Windows' Task List).

- If you're looking for your Windows programs, they're hiding in a folder called WIN-OS/2 Groups. Inside this folder, you'll find another folder for each of the program groups you used in Windows. For example, you might find a folder for a program group called Microsoft Office.

A Note About HPFS

HPFS is short for the High Performance File System, which you can install when you install OS/2 if you want. If you choose to install HPFS, you can give files long descriptive file names using up to 254 characters that make your files easier to identify. The more common FAT file system (short for file allocation table) that DOS and Windows use limits you to a meager eight-plus-three characters for naming files.

Being able to use long file names is not the only reason to install HPFS. HPFS is faster and more efficient than the older FAT systems. In addition, HPFS adds useful tidbits, called *extended attributes*, to each file. Extended attributes describe things about the file, such as when it was created and the name of the program in which it was created.

There is a downside to HPFS, too. In order to install it, you must wipe out all the data on your PC (you can copy it back after installation).

Why You Need This Book

This *10 Minute Guide* teaches you only what you need to know to use OS/2 Warp, without a lot of technical details you don't want to know or don't have time to learn. Each lesson is designed to take only ten minutes to complete, and because each lesson is self-contained, you can go straight to the features you want to know about, starting and stopping wherever you like. You learn what you need to know when you need to know it, and you progress at your own pace.

How This Book Is Organized

Each of the short lessons in the *10 Minute Guide* includes step-by-step instructions for performing some specific task. The following special icons also appear as a means of helping you quickly identify particular types of information:

Timesaver Tip icons offer shortcuts and hints for using the program efficiently.

Plain English icons define new terms.

Panic Button icons appear where new users often run into trouble.

Special Tips for Windows Users provide extra information for users switching from Microsoft Windows 3.1.

The following conventions have been used to clarify the steps you must perform:

On-screen text	Any text that appears on-screen is shown in bold.
What you select	Menus, commands, and options you need to select appear in color.
What you type	The information you type appears in bold and color.
Commands and Options	The names of menus, commands, buttons, and dialog boxes are shown with the first letter capitalized for easy recognition.
Key+Key Combinations	In many cases, you must press a two-key key combination (such as Ctrl+X) to issue a command. In such cases, hold down the first key (Ctrl) and press the second key (X).

Acknowledgments

Thanks to my teammates at Que for their contributions to this book: Faithe Wempen, Mark Enochs, Audra Gable, Herb Feltner, and our great production team.

Trademarks

All terms mentioned in this book that are known to be or are suspected of being trademarks or service marks have been appropriately capitalized. Que Corporation cannot attest to the accuracy of this information. Use of a term in this book should not be regarded as affecting the validity of any trademark or service mark.

Lesson 1

Starting OS/2 Warp

In this lesson, you'll learn how to start OS/2 Warp and how the parts of the Warp screen are organized.

Starting OS/2 Warp

OS/2 Warp, like DOS, is an *operating system*. An operating system controls the functions of your PC. The process of starting an operating system is called *booting*. Once you've installed the program, you can boot (or start) any operating system, including Warp, by just turning on the PC.

However, there are other ways to boot (or start) OS/2:

- You normally start OS/2 by just turning on the computer.

- If you installed OS/2 with the Boot Manager option, you need to choose your operating system from a list each time.

- If you installed OS/2 with the Dual Boot option, it's possible to boot to DOS (start the DOS operating system) instead of booting to OS/2. However, if you do this, your PC boots to DOS from then on, until you tell it to reboot to OS/2.

The following sections fill you in on the details of each of these methods.

Starting OS/2 Normally

As I said, all you normally have to do to start OS/2 is turn on
the PC. (If you encounter a DOS prompt or a menu when
starting OS/2, see the upcoming sections for help.) When
you start OS/2, it begins to prepare itself for the day. At one
point, it displays a clock cursor, which gives you something
to look at while it colors in the rest of your Desktop. Eventually, the start-up process ends, and your screen looks something like Figure 1.1.

Why Is My Screen Different?   Your screen
will be lacking a few elements if you don't have
Windows or if you didn't install all the programs
on the BonusPak.

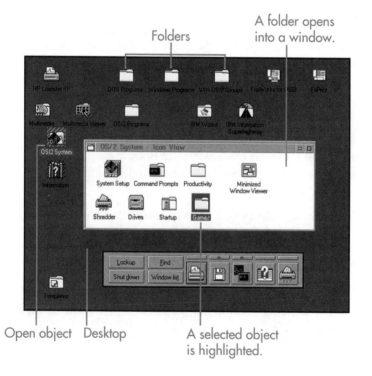

Figure 1.1   Welcome to OS/2 Warp.

Starting OS/2 with the Boot Manager Option

If you don't see OS/2 when you start the PC, it could be that you installed something called *Boot Manager*. If so, you need to select the operating system you want to use from the menu that appears when you turn on the PC. To do so, follow these steps:

> **Boot Manager** One of the Advanced installation options, which allows you to keep multiple operating systems (DOS, OS/2 2/1, OS/2 Warp, and so on) on the same PC. With Boot Manager, you choose which operating system to use every time you start your PC.

1. Turn on the PC.

2. When the selection menu appears, use the arrow keys to select the option OS/2 Warp.

3. Press Enter. You should see the OS/2 Desktop (see Figure 1.1).

Starting OS/2 with the Dual Boot Option

If you installed *Dual Boot* (which you did if you installed OS/2 using the Easy option), OS/2 should start when you turn on the PC. If it doesn't, you somehow left it booted to DOS (in other words, you started your computer with DOS—and not OS/2—the last time). So now you're looking at a DOS prompt (**C:\>**). Here's how to get back to OS/2:

> **Dual Boot** The default installation option, which enables you to boot to either DOS or OS/2 Warp, depending on your needs.

1. At the DOS prompt, type C:\OS2\BOOT /OS2.

2. Press Enter. The PC restarts and boots OS/2.

Starting DOS with the Dual Boot Option

With the Dual Boot option, it's possible to restart your PC
with DOS. For example, you might want to boot to DOS to
run a DOS program (such as a flight simulator game) that
doesn't run properly under OS/2. To boot to DOS from
within Warp:

1. Double-click on the OS/2 System folder.

2. Select the Command Prompts folder.

3. Double-click on the Dual Boot icon.

How Warp Is Organized

In OS/2 Warp, your screen is set up like a desktop. Like a
real desktop, your OS/2 screen is cluttered with objects that
serve special purposes. On your real desktop, you probably
have a telephone, a notepad, a computer, and maybe a
printer. In OS/2, the things that clutter your Desktop are
called *objects* (although if you're a former Windows user,
you might know them as icons). Each part of your PC (the
hard disk, the printer, your programs, and your files) is
represented by an object. To do anything in OS/2, you
manipulate these objects.

**Windows Uses Icons (Objects),
Too** That's true, but in Windows, those
icons represent programs only. In OS/2,
these object-icons represent everything,
including your programs, your files, and the parts of
your computer (such as the printer and the hard disk).

OS/2 has four types of objects: *data-file objects* (which represent the things you create, like letters and such), *program objects* (which represent your programs, such as your word processor and your spreadsheet), *device objects* (which represent parts of the computer, like the printer and the hard disk), and *folder objects* (which are gathering places for other objects). You can usually tell which of these categories an object fits into by how it looks. For example, folder objects usually look like manila folders (although they sometimes look different, as does the Information folder shown in Figure 1.1). Figure 1.2 shows one of each type of object. Look for these object types as you explore OS/2 Warp.

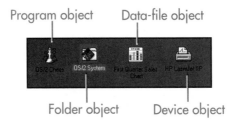

Figure 1.2   The different types of objects you'll encounter.

You organize objects by placing them in folders, and you can even place folders within other larger folders for further organization. To see what's inside a folder, you open it into a *window*, a box that surrounds similar elements on-screen (see Figure 1.1).

Folders are the visual representation of *directories*, which are used to organize *files* on the hard disk. For example, when you move a data-file object (such as a memo or a letter) from one folder to another, you are moving the file it's associated with to a different directory on the hard disk.

Directories and Files   OS/2 stores information in *files*. Anything—a letter, a graphic
image, even the instructions for a program—
can be stored in a file. Files are organized on
the hard disk within *directories*, which are like the
drawers in a large filing cabinet. Keeping files in
directories with other related files makes it easier to
locate and work with files.

**Are Folders Like Program
Groups?**   Yes and no. Like Windows'
program groups, folders contain various
object-icons, but in Windows, a program
group can contain only program icons. In Warp, a
folder can contain a program icon, a data-file icon, a
device icon, and even another folder. This helps you
keep related programs and data-files together and
organized.

In this lesson, you learned how to start OS/2, and you
learned how it is organized. In the next lesson, you'll get a
quick tour of OS/2 and you'll learn to use a mouse.

Lesson

A Quick Tour of OS/2 Warp

In this lesson, you'll learn about the main features of OS/2 and their functions and how to use a mouse.

Getting to Know OS/2 Warp

When you first start OS/2, your screen looks something like Figure 2.1.

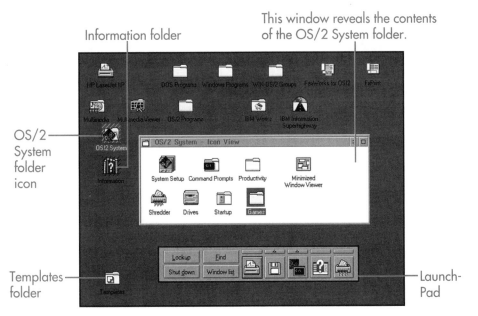

Information folder

This window reveals the contents of the OS/2 System folder.

OS/2 System folder icon

Templates folder

Launch-Pad

Figure 2.1 Ready for a tour?

In the following sections, I'll take you on a quick tour of OS/2 Warp so you can get to know a little bit more about it. You'll learn who the major players are and what functions they perform.

The OS/2 System Folder

The heart of OS/2 is stuffed into a folder called OS/2 System, which you'll find conveniently open for you on the Desktop. There's too much in this folder to cover completely here, but here's a glimpse of what you'll find in future lessons:

- Inside the System Setup folder, you'll find objects you can use to customize OS/2. Jump to Lesson 24 for more information.

- The Command Prompts folder provides access to a DOS prompt, an OS/2 prompt, and Windows. See Lesson 19 for help.

> **How Do I Start Windows?**   If you want to start up Windows, just open the Command Prompts folder and select the WIN-OS/2 Full Screen object. Keep in mind that you don't have to start Windows to start a Windows program (all of which are kept in the WIN-OS/2 Groups folder on the Desktop). See Lesson 19.

- The Productivity folder contains the OS/2 Warp *freebies*, the free programs, such as a picture viewer and a simple text editor, that come with OS/2. The BonusPak applications are stored in their own folders.

- When you minimize a window to get it out of your way, OS/2 places its icon in the Minimized Window Viewer folder. Open this folder to redisplay a previously minimized window. See Lesson 5 for more info.

**Minimized Windows Aren't at the
Bottom of the Screen?**   Right. If you're
a former Windows user, remembering to
open the Minimized Window Viewer to
locate windows you've minimized will take some getting
used to. You won't find the minimized icons at the
bottom of the OS/2 Desktop.

- Use the Shredder to delete unwanted objects from the Desktop. However, since the Shredder also appears on the LaunchPad, you don't have to open the OS/2 System folder to find it. See Lesson 9 for help.

- The Drives folder provides access to all drives, such as the hard disk (C:) and the diskette drives (A: and B:). Some drives are also accessible through the LaunchPad. See Lesson 13.

- The Startup folder contains the programs you want to launch when you start OS/2. Place your favorite programs in the Startup folder, and they will start automatically for you each day. See Lesson 15 for info.

- The Games folder contains free entertainment, courtesy of OS/2.

Information Folder

Inside the Information folder is the OS/2 tutorial, which you might have taken after installing OS/2. If you want to run the tutorial now, see Lesson 4 for help. You'll also find a Master Help Index icon in the Information folder. You use the Master Help Index to open a section of help about a particular subject, which is useful when you know the name of the thing you need help with. There's also a Glossary icon, which you can use to look up OS/2 terms like "extended attributes" and "metafile." There are additional icons for specialized help areas such as "Printing in OS/2" and "Windows Programs in OS/2." You'll find out more about the Help system in Lesson 4.

Templates Folder

The Templates folder contains templates for creating new objects. A *template* is like a form you fill in to create a new version of the template object. For example, there's a template for creating new folders, text files, spreadsheets, charts, and other items. The idea is that you select the correct template for the object you want to create (such as a letter or a chart), and you're guided through the process of creating the new object. See Lesson 17 for more help.

LaunchPad

One thing on the Desktop that you can't miss is OS/2's newest item: the LaunchPad. It keeps the objects you use the most close by, where they belong. The LaunchPad contains many of the objects you'll use daily, such as the Printer object (for printing), the Shredder (for deleting objects), and the Drive A object (for looking at the contents of a diskette). In addition, there are buttons for switching between programs, locking up your PC while you take a quick break, locating a missing icon, and shutting down. You can add additional objects to the LaunchPad to customize it for your own use; see Lesson 16 for help.

Using a Mouse

To tell OS/2 what to do, you select, move, open, and close objects (among other things). All of these tasks are easy to do with a mouse. You'll begin using the mouse in the next lesson, so if you're not familiar with it, take the time now to learn how to use it.

There are four basic ways to use a mouse:

- **To point to an object with the mouse,** move the on-screen pointer (the mouse pointer) on top of an object by moving the mouse in the same direction on the mouse pad. The tip of the mouse pointer arrow must touch the object to "point" to it.

- **To click on an object with the mouse,** point to the object with the mouse pointer and press the left mouse button once. Sometimes you use the right mouse button to click; this is called right-clicking.

- **To double-click on an object,** point to that object with the mouse pointer and press the left mouse button twice very quickly.

- **To drag an object,** point to that object with the mouse pointer and click the right mouse button. Continue to hold down the right mouse button as you move the mouse. The object moves with the pointer as you drag it. When you get to the location where you want to "drop" the object, release the right button.

In this lesson, you learned about the main features of OS/2 and how to use a mouse. In the next lesson, you'll learn how to shut down OS/2 at the end of the day.

Lesson

Shutting Down OS/2 Warp

In this lesson, you'll learn how to shut down OS/2 Warp when you're finished with it and how to lock your system when you're going to be away from your desk for a short period.

Shutting Down at the End of the Day

When you reach the end of a long day, don't just flip the off switch. You need to shut down OS/2 properly, which means that you've got to give OS/2 Warp a chance to put its stuff away and to save your work. To shut down OS/2 properly:

1. Save any open documents. (Turn to Lesson 17 for help.)

2. Close any programs you have running. (See Lesson 15 for more info.) You can leave some programs and folders open if you want as long as you've saved your data; OS/2 will reopen these objects for you automatically the next time you start your PC.

3. Click on the Shut down button on the LaunchPad (see Figure 3.1). If the LaunchPad is not visible, double-click within any open window to bring it into view.

Click here to
shut down.

Figure 3.1   The Shut down button.

4. You'll see a message asking you to confirm that you want to continue the shut down process. Click on OK to continue or Cancel to return to OS/2.

5. If you left any programs running (didn't close them down), you'll have one last chance to save your data. Click on No to return to OS/2 so you can close down the programs and save your data. Click on Yes to continue the shut down process; however, this may cause you to lose some work if you haven't already saved it.

6. When you see the message telling you it's okay to turn off the PC, go ahead and do so by flipping the power switch.

> **Alternative Shutdown**   Another way to shut down is to place the mouse pointer in an empty place on the Desktop and right-click. From the pop-up menu that appears, select Shut down. Click on OK to continue the shut down process or click on Cancel to return to OS/2.

Shutting Down After a Crash

Sometimes you'll be working with several programs, just minding your own business, when a program will lock up (*crash*) and refuse to acknowledge your commands. If this happens, the first thing you should do is try to shut down the bad program using these steps:

1. Click on the Window list button on the LaunchPad
   or double-click with both mouse buttons on a free
   area of the Desktop to display the Window list (see
   Figure 3.2).

Select the program
you want to terminate.

Figure 3.2   Use the Window list to shut down an errant
program.

2. Select the locked-up program.

3. Force the program to shut down by pressing Delete.
   (You will lose any unsaved work.)

> **Display the Window List**   OS/2's
> Window list (like Windows' Task List) keeps
> track of all the currently open windows. You
> use it as you would the Task List in Win-
> dows: to switch from window to window and to termi-
> nate (close) a window. In Windows, you can press
> Ctrl+Esc to display the Task List. You can also press
> Ctrl+Esc to display the Window list in OS/2.

    If you can't get your locked-up program to respond,
you'll need to give the PC a "push start" (technically called a
reboot) to clear the problem so you can later restart the
program. Because rebooting causes any unsaved data to be
lost, you'll need to shut down any other programs you may
have running and save your data before you reboot. Follow
these steps to do just that:

1. Click on the Window list button on the LaunchPad or double-click with both mouse buttons on a free area of the Desktop to display the Window list. Then switch to a working program by double-clicking on its name.

2. Save your data and shut down the program.

3. Repeat steps 1 and 2 as necessary to shut down each of your *working* programs. (Since you can't get your locked-up program to respond, forget about it for now.)

4. When you've shut down all the programs you can, reboot by pressing Ctrl+Alt+Delete at the same time. If the computer does not restart, you'll have to perform a *cold boot* by turning the PC off, waiting a few moments, and turning it back on again.

What's Going On Here?   When you restart your computer, OS/2 will attempt to restart the locked-up program, which may in turn cause the program to lock up again. If you find yourself in this cycle of crash-reboot-crash-reboot, restart OS/2, but this time, when you see the clock, press and hold Ctrl+Shift+F1. This tells OS/2 to stop trying to reload open programs. You must hold down the keys until OS/2 completes the start-up process.

Locking Your System Temporarily

If you're just leaving your desk for lunch or a meeting and you want to protect your data without shutting down, you can lock your system. This prevents anyone from using your PC while you're gone. The following steps show you how to lock up:

1. Click on the Lockup button on the LaunchPad (see Figure 3.3), or display the Desktop pop-up menu (by clicking with the right button on an open spot on the Desktop) and select Lockup now.

Click here to lock up.

Figure 3.3 The Lockup button.

2. Type a password of up to 15 characters. Because OS/2 distinguishes between upper- and lowercase letters, "Secret" is different from "secret" or "SECRET."

3. Press Tab and type your password again. (For security reasons, your password does not appear on-screen as you type.)

4. Click on OK to lock your system. The OS/2 logo is displayed on your screen until you unlock or restart your system.

To unlock your system, simply type your password and press Enter. You'll be returned to the Desktop.

I Forgot My Password! If you can't remember your password, just turn the PC off and then back on to restart OS/2. If you want to prevent others from being able to bypass the security so easily, display the Desktop pop-up menu and select Settings. Click on the notebook tab called Lockup. Under Timeout, click on the Lock on startup option. Close the notebook by double-clicking on the title-bar icon. Of course, now you have to make sure you know your password!

By the way, OS/2 remembers your password, so the next time you want to lock up, all you have to do is click on the Lockup button. It'll lock up for you immediately without you having to type anything.

If you want to change the password later on, follow these steps:

1. Display the Desktop pop-up menu by right-clicking on the Desktop.

2. Click on Settings.

3. Click on the notebook tab called Lockup.

4. Turn to page three of the Lockup section by clicking two times on the right arrow button at the bottom of the page.

5. Enter your new password as before, and then click on OK.

6. Close the Settings notebook by double-clicking on the title-bar icon in the upper left-hand corner.

If you want to display something other than the OS/2 logo when you lock up, just follow the steps above to open the Settings notebook, and on page two of the Lockup section, select another file under Image.

Using the Lockup Feature as a Screen Saver

You can set the Lockup feature to act as a *screen saver* if you'd like. Here's what you do:

Screen Saver A *screen saver* is a program that prevents images from burning into your PC's "retina" (the monitor) by displaying a constantly moving image.

1. Display the Desktop pop-up menu by right-clicking on the Desktop.

2. Click on Settings.

3. Click on the Lockup notebook tab.

4. Select the Auto-dim option.

5. Close the Settings notebook by double-clicking on the title-bar icon.

When you lock up your system, OS/2 displays its logo, blanks the screen for a moment, and then displays a floating lock. (The lock moves around the screen, creating a constantly changing display.) To unlock the system, type your password and press Enter.

In this lesson, you learned how to shut down your system safely and lock your system to prevent intruders. In the next lesson, you'll learn how to use the OS/2 Warp Help system.

Lesson

Getting Help

In this lesson, you'll learn how to get help when you need it.

Starting Help

For the easiest way to access the Help system, follow these steps:

1. Select what you want help on. For example, click on an object or a menu item.

2. Press F1.

For example, if you were looking in the OS/2 System folder wondering what the Startup folder icon was for, you could select the Startup folder and then press F1 for help. You'd see a dialog box similar to the one in Figure 4.1.

You can get help by pressing the F1 key regardless of where you are. As a matter of fact, most programs (including OS/2, Windows, and DOS programs) reserve the F1 key for Help. So just press F1 when you need assistance in completing some task.

In a moment, you'll learn how to navigate within the Help system, but first, I'll show you some other ways to get help.

Select the Startup folder   ...and you get this
and press F1...   Help window.

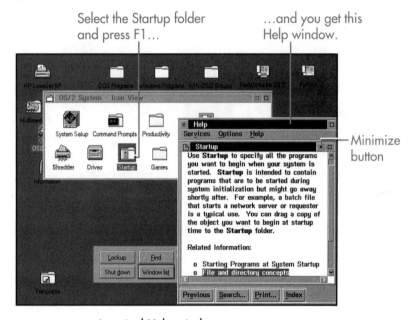

Figure 4.1 A typical Help window.

Accessing the Master Help Index

The Master Help Index is simply an alphabetical listing of all
the topics covered within Help. So if you want help on a
particular task or topic, you can access the Master Help
Index and navigate to the particular Help section you need.
(This method is not as simple and straightforward as pressing
F1, so you probably won't use it as much.)

1. Open the Information folder by double-clicking on it.

2. Double-click on the Master Help Index icon. The
   Master Help Index, shown in Figure 4.2, appears.

3. Press the first letter in the topic you want to look
   up, or click on the appropriate tab. If necessary,
   scroll to the tab you need. For example, to view the
   topic *LaunchPad*, press L or scroll to the L tab and
   click on it.

Double-click on a
topic to view it.

Click on a tab to jump to that
section of the Master Help Index.

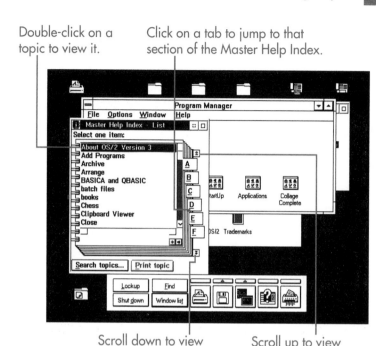

Scroll down to view
more index tabs.

Scroll up to view
more index tabs.

Figure 4.2   The Master Help Index.

4. Double-click on the topic you want to view, and
you'll be taken to that section in Help. For example,
double-click on the word LaunchPad in the L
section of the index.

> **Get to the Index Fast**   If you press F1 to get
> help on a particular topic, you can switch to
> another topic by clicking on the Index button (see
> Figure 4.1). This takes you to the Master Help
> Index (see Figure 4.2).

Accessing Help from the Command Prompt

If you prefer to, you can type commands at the OS/2 command prompt instead of manipulating objects from within the Desktop. (You'll learn more about the OS/2 command prompt in Lesson 19.) If you're working from the command prompt and you encounter an error message such as

SYS0021: The drive is not ready.

you can get help on the error message by typing HELP SYS0021 at the prompt and pressing Enter. You'll see something like this:

SYS0021: The drive is not ready.

EXPLANATION: One of the following errors occurred:
o The drive is empty.
o The drive door is open.
o The drive is in use.

ACTION: Do one of the following and retry the command:
o Insert a diskette in the drive.
o Close the drive door.
o Wait until the drive is available.

Follow the on-screen instructions, and the error message should go away.

Accessing Other Parts of Help

The OS/2 Help system comprises many sections, including a comprehensive Master Index, a Glossary, and a Tutorial. You will learn how to use each of these features in this lesson. Although there are other parts to the OS/2 Help system, they are more specialized, providing help for increasing performance, printing, using Windows, and using multimedia. To locate these special help sections, open the Information

folder and double-click on an icon for the section you want
to start up.

Navigating Help

Whether you access the Help system by pressing F1 or by
using the Master Help Index, here are some tips for getting
to the information you need:

* Press Page Up or Page Down or use the scroll
  arrows to view the rest of your topic.

* Blue words are *hypertext*. Double-click on a
  hypertext word to jump to a different section of
  Help or to see a definition for the blue word.

* Click on Previous to return to the last page you saw.

* Press Ctrl+H to see a history of all the pages you've
  viewed; double-click on a page in the history list to
  jump back to that page.

* Click on Index to access the Master Help Index.

* Press Ctrl+C for the Table of Contents.

* If you find something you want to keep, print it out.
  Just click on the Print button, select what you want
  to print, and click on Print again.

* Click on Search, type a word, click on All sections,
  and then click on Search again to locate a specific
  topic. (Figure 4.3 shows the Search dialog box that
  appears.) Once the search list appears, double-click
  on a topic to jump to it.

> **How Do I Return to Search?**   When you
> select a topic from the search list, if that topic is
> not the right one, you can return to the search list
> to select another topic. Just click on the Minimize
> button (shown in Figure 4.1), and you'll see the missing
> search list.

Select a section to search. — Type something to search for.

Click here to start the search.

Figure 4.3 Use Search to quickly locate a topic.

Use a Wild Card for Quick Searches
Ordinarily, Search looks only for an exact match of what you type. However, you can widen the search by including a wild card. For example, add the asterisk (*) at the end of the word *print* (such as *print**), and Search finds any text string that starts with *print*: print, printer, printing, and so on.

Using the Glossary

When OS/2 throws a technical word at you (such as piping, attribute, DBCS, or data-file object), you can find out what it means by using the Help system's Glossary, which contains a list of words and their definitions. To open the Glossary:

1. Double-click on the Information folder to open it.

2. Double-click on the Glossary icon.

3. Type the first letter of the word you're looking for, or click on the appropriate letter tab. If necessary, scroll to the tab you need. For example, to find a definition of the word *piping*, press P or scroll to the P tab and click on it.

4. Double-click on a word to see its definition. On the right side of the screen, OS/2 displays the definition of the selected word, as shown in Figure 4.4.

Click on a letter tab to view words
beginning with that letter.

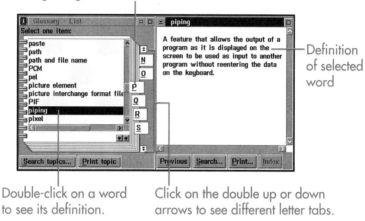

Double-click on a word
to see its definition.

Click on the double up or down
arrows to see different letter tabs.

Figure 4.4   Use the Glossary to locate a definition for
a word.

Using the Tutorial

If you skipped the tutorial when you installed OS/2, you can
still get back to it at any time. To do so, simply follow these
steps:

1. Click once on the Tutorial button on the
   LaunchPad, or open the Information folder and
   double-click on the Tutorial icon.

2. When the tutorial starts, click once on the right
   arrow button; you'll see the main Tutorial screen,
   shown in Figure 4.5.

3. Read the introduction, and then click the right
   arrow button once more. Now you're in the OS/2
   Basics section.

4. If you'd like, select a different topic to view using one of these methods:

- Switch to another section by clicking on one of the subjects listed on the left.

- Double-click on a subject in the blue list on the right to jump to that topic within the OS/2 Basics section.

Choose a subject from this list.

Double-click here to jump to a specific topic.

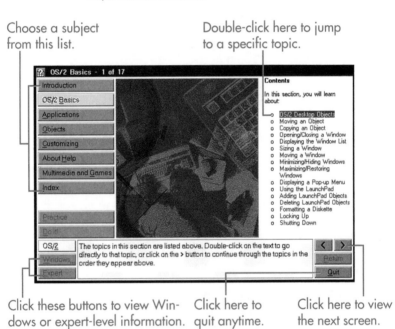

Click these buttons to view Windows or expert-level information.

Click here to quit anytime.

Click here to view the next screen.

Figure 4.5 Welcome to the OS/2 Tutorial.

5. Once you've picked your topic, click on the right arrow button to move through it. Click on the left arrow button to go back. For further information on the selected topic, try these options:

- Click on the Windows button to see this topic compared to the same thing in Windows. (This can be helpful for former Windows users.)

- Click on the Expert button to see detailed information on this topic.

- Click on the Practice button when it lights up, and you'll get a chance to test your skills. If you'd rather see someone else do it first, click on Do it!.

6. When you're ready to leave the tutorial, click on Quit and (if necessary) click on Yes. To get back to the main screen from a practice session, click on Return.

In this lesson, you learned how to access the various parts of the Help system. In the next lesson, you'll learn how to work with windows.

Lesson

Working with OS/2 Windows

In this lesson, you'll learn how to open, close, and resize windows in OS/2.

Opening and Closing Windows

In OS/2, a window is simply a container for something. For example, when you start a program, its tools, its menus, and your work are placed within a window. The window defines the program's outer boundaries and separates it from other things on-screen. Windows are not used only with programs; for example, a folder is just a collection of objects placed in a window. All windows have lots of parts, as shown in Figure 5.1.

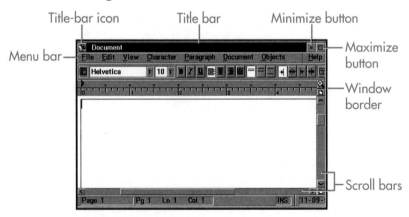

Figure 5.1 The parts of a window.

To open a window:

1. Place the mouse pointer on an object (icon).

2. Double-click the left mouse button.

So, for example, to open a program's window (which is the same as starting the program), just double-click on the program's icon. To open a folder, double-click on its icon.

When you open certain windows, such as a folder window, it opens in *icon view*, which means that its contents are displayed with pictures instead of words. But when you're dealing with files, you may want to open a file window in another view. See Lesson 6 for help.

To close a window:

1. Place the mouse pointer on the title-bar icon.

2. Double-click the left mouse button.

What About the Exit Command?   If you're trying to close a program window, you should select the Exit command (if it exists) instead of double-clicking the title-bar icon. (This lets the program know that OS/2 is shutting it down, and the program can then remind you to save your data.) Although you can always use the title-bar icon to close a window, using the Exit command for Windows and DOS programs gives you an extra measure of safety. Just click on the File menu to open it, and then click on Exit.

Closing Lots of Windows at Once   To close multiple windows at once, first display the Window list by clicking on the Window list button on the LaunchPad or by clicking both mouse buttons on a free area of the Desktop. (You can also display the Window list by pressing Ctrl+Esc.) Select the windows you want to close by pressing Ctrl and clicking on them. Then close them all by pressing Delete.

Moving Windows

If a window is in your way, you can move it to the side. If you move a window over part of another window, it stays on top, covering part of that other window. To move a window, you drag it with the left or right mouse button, as described here.

1. Click on the title bar of the window you want to move to select it.

2. Continue to hold down the mouse button, and drag the window to wherever you want it. (A ghostly window frame follows your movement so you'll know where to drop the window.)

3. Release the mouse button.

Why Can't I Move Objects the Same Way?   You can use the left or the right mouse button to move a window; however, you *must* use the right button to move an object. For that reason, you might want to use the right mouse button every time you drag, whether you're moving an object or a window.

Minimizing, Maximizing, and Resizing Windows

You can change the size of a window to whatever size makes it the easiest to work with. When you maximize a window, it fills the screen; when you minimize a window, it shrinks down out of view. If you want to make the window a size somewhere between those two, you can resize it to your own precise specifications.

Minimizing a Window

To minimize a window, click on its Minimize button, which
is located on the top right side of the window. (The Minimize button looks like a small square. See Figure 5.1.) When
you minimize a window, it shrinks to an icon and tucks itself
away in the Minimized Window Viewer, a special folder-
window into which OS/2 places all your minimized windows
so they're out of the way and in one spot. Figure 5.2 shows
the Minimized Window Viewer with three minimized windows in it.

Figure 5.2   The Minimized Window Viewer.

This Isn't Like Windows!   When you
minimize a window in OS/2, it is hidden
inside the Minimized Window Viewer. This is
unlike Microsoft Windows, where minimized
windows are lined up like tokens at the bottom of the
screen. However, if you want, you can make OS/2
mimic that Windows behavior. To do so, right-click
anywhere on the Desktop and select Settings. Click on
the Window tab, select Minimize button, and select
Minimize window to desktop. Then close the notebook
by double-clicking on its title-bar icon.

To restore a minimized window, open the OS/2 System
folder and double-click on the Minimized Window Viewer.
Locate your window's icon in the Minimized Window
Viewer and double-click on it to redisplay the window. You
might want to drag the Minimized Window Viewer icon onto
the Desktop or to the LaunchPad for easier access to your
minimized windows.

Some windows have a Hide button instead of a Minimize button. The Hide button, shown in Figure 5.3, looks like four dots set in the pattern of a square. If present, the Hide button is located where the Minimize button would normally be, in the top right corner of a window. When you click on the Hide button, the window is not placed in the Minimized Window Viewer; instead, it is hidden completely until you display it with Window List. (You'll learn how to use the Window List in a moment.)

Figure 5.3   The Hide button takes the place of the Minimize button in some windows.

Why Two Buttons?   Each window contains either a Minimize button or a Hide button, but never both. That's because some windows can only be hidden, and not minimized. Just remember that if a window has a Hide button, the window will not appear in the Minimized Window Viewer, only on the Window list.

You can use the Window list to restore a minimized window or a hidden window. Display the Window list by clicking on the Window list button on the LaunchPad, by clicking with both mouse buttons on an open area of the Desktop, or by pressing Ctrl+Esc. Locate your window's name in the list and double-click on it to redisplay the window.

Maximizing a Window

When you maximize a window, the window spreads out to fill up the screen—at least sometimes. When you maximize a DOS program running in a window (instead of full screen) it fills up about two-thirds of the window.

This Isn't the Way Windows Does It
That's right. When you maximize a window
under MS Windows, it fills the screen,
regardless of whether or not it's a DOS
window. Under OS/2, you must either resize the DOS
window manually if you want it to fill the screen or
change the object's settings so that it runs in a full-screen
session. To change the object's settings, right-click on the
DOS program's icon, select Settings, and then click on
the Session tab. Select DOS full screen, and then close
the Settings notebook.

To maximize a window, click on its Maximize button,
located in the upper right-hand corner of the window (see
Figure 5.1). Once a window is maximized, the Maximize
button is replaced with a Restore button that looks like
Figure 5.4. Click on the Restore button to restore the maximized window to its former size.

Figure 5.4 A maximized window has a Restore button.

Maximizing Quickly You can maximize a
window quickly by double-clicking on its title bar.

Resizing a Window

You can resize a window manually to any size that works for
you. To resize a window:

1. Move the mouse pointer very slowly to the
   window's border. When you reach a certain point,
   the mouse pointer turns into a double-headed arrow.

2. Now press and hold down the left mouse button.

3. While you're holding the mouse button down, drag the edge outward to make the window bigger or inward to make it smaller. You see a ghostly image of the window edge as you drag (see Figure 5.5). As long as you hold the mouse button down, you can play with the window's size as long as you want.

4. When you've got the window "just right," release the mouse button. The window is resized.

You see a ghostly window border as you drag.┐

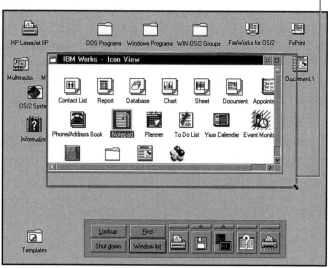

Figure 5.5 Drag the window's border to resize a window.

Remember these resizing tips:

• Drag a window's corner to resize it both vertically and horizontally at the same time.

• If a window is maximized so that it fills your screen, you won't be able to resize it manually because it won't have a border. Click on the Restore button to restore the window to its previous size, and then resize it manually if necessary.

Using Scroll Bars

If you resize a window so that its contents are not completely visible, scroll bars appear. These guidelines teach you how to use scroll bars:

- To see more of the window's contents, click on the up or down arrows on the scroll bar, as shown in Figure 5.6. This will move you one "line" at a time.

- Click between the scroll box and the scroll arrow to move one windowful at a time.

- Drag the scroll box along the scroll bar to move a corresponding distance within the window. For example, if you drag the scroll box halfway down the scroll bar, you'll move to the middle of the document.

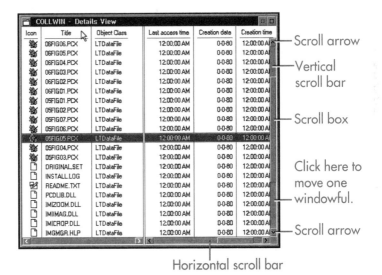

Figure 5.6 Scroll bars let you view information not currently visible in the window.

The Scroll Bar Looks Different Unlike
in Microsoft Windows, the scroll box in
OS/2 indicates approximately how much of
the total window's contents you're seeing.
For example, if you're seeing half of the contents of a
window, the scroll box fills half of the scroll bar. This is
different from the way it works in Windows 3.1, where
the scroll box is the same size in every window, regardless of how much of the file you're seeing.

In this lesson, you learned how to open, close, minimize, maximize, and resize windows. In the next lesson,
you'll learn other things you can do with windows, such
as arranging their contents and changing their views.

6

More on Working with Windows

In this lesson, you'll learn how to arrange windows and icons, change a window's view, and switch from window to window.

Arranging Windows

If you work in OS/2 for extended periods of time and open lots of windows, the time will come when you need to restore some type of order. You can display your open windows on the Desktop in one of two arrangements: *cascading*, in which each window overlaps the next (much like you'd hold a hand of cards), or *tiled*, in which each window takes up exactly the same amount of space horizontally across the screen.

To arrange your open windows, follow these steps:

1. Click on the Window list button on the LaunchPad, or click both buttons on the Desktop, or press Ctrl+Esc.

2. Press and hold the Ctrl key and click on the windows you want to rearrange.

3. Right-click anywhere on the Desktop and select Tile or Cascade from the menu that appears.

> **Don't Select That!**   When you're selecting
> windows to rearrange in the Window list, don't
> select Desktop-Icon View. You can't rearrange the
> Desktop as if it were a window; it takes up the
> entire screen. For that matter, you probably don't want
> to select LaunchPad-Palette, either. Instead of arranging
> the LaunchPad with the other windows, you'll want to
> leave the LaunchPad where it is.

Arranging Icons Within a Window

You can restore order to the icons within a window, too. To
do so, right-click inside the folder window and select Arrange
from the pop-up menu that appears. Your icons will snap into
an orderly arrangement.

You control how objects are arranged with the settings
under the View tab of the Settings notebook. Normally, this
is set to Non-grid, which means that icons stay where you
put them until you select the Arrange command. If you
change the setting from Non-grid to Flowed, all your objects
are arranged into neat columns and rows. If you select Non-
flowed, all your objects are arranged automatically in a single
column.

> **What If I Don't Like It?**   If you don't like the
> new arrangement, simply right-click inside the
> folder window again and select Undo arrange
> from the pop-up menu.

Here's how to change the setting for the icon
arrangement:

1. Right-click inside the folder window.

2. From the menu that appears, select Settings.

3. Click on the View tab.

4. Select an option: Non-grid, Flowed, or Non-flowed.

This changes the default icon arrangement for that one window *only*. Repeat for additional windows.

Changing a Window's View

Windows have three views: Icon, Tree, and Detail, as shown in Figure 6.1. Icon view displays the contents of the window as icons, or pictures. Tree view depicts the window's contents in folders (directories), but does not show individual files. Detail view displays the window's contents as a list of files along with their creation dates and sizes and displays folders for subdirectories (if there are any, of course).

Where Are the Files?   Tree view doesn't show the contents of a directory, just the folders (directories) themselves. So if you want to know what files you have in the root (main) directory on your disk, don't choose Tree view.

All windows have a default view. To open a window in the default view, simply double-click on its icon. Folder windows and windows that display the files on a diskette, open automatically in Icon view. Some windows open in other views; for example, if you open a window on a hard disk, you'll see the files listed in Tree view.

Before you open a window, you should decide which view you want to use because you *can't* change a window's view once it is open. You can only open *another* window with a different view.

Tree view

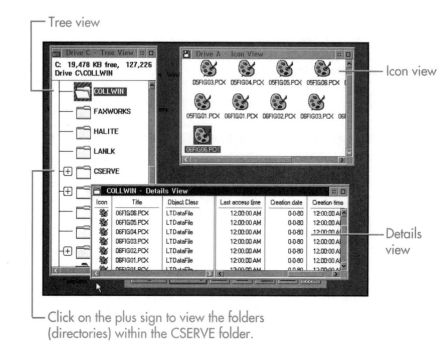

Icon view

Details view

Click on the plus sign to view the folders (directories) within the CSERVE folder.

Figure 6.1 Different window views.

To open a window in a particular view instead of the default view, follow these steps:

1. Right-click on the object. For example, right-click on a folder icon.

2. From the menu that appears, click on the arrow next to Open.

3. Select your view from the list.

In Tree view, when a folder has a folder inside it (in other words, a directory has subdirectories in it), a little plus sign appears in front of the folder. Click on the plus sign (+) to open the folder/directory and show the folders/ subdirectories inside it. Click on the minus sign (–) to hide them.

Displaying Files With File Manager you can change the sort order and level of detail in a window without opening a new window. However, in OS/2, if you open a window on a disk, you can't change its view; you have to open a different window with another view.

Tree view, by the way, is similar to the left-hand side of the Windows File Manager; Detail view is like the right-hand side of File Manager.

Switching from Window to Window

The window you're currently working in is called the *active window*. It's easy to tell which window is the active one: its title bar is darker than all the other open windows. (The default color for the active window title bar is purple.)

There are two ways to switch to another window (and make it the active one):

- Click anywhere inside a window to activate it. Activating a window brings it to the top of the open-window pile, making it easier to work with.

- If you can't see the window you want to activate, click on the Window list button on the LaunchPad or press Ctrl+Esc to display the Window list. Then double-click on the window you want to switch to (make active).

In this lesson, you learned how to arrange windows and icons. You also learned how to switch from one window to another and to change window views. In the next lesson, you'll learn how to use menus and dialog boxes.

Lesson

Using Menus and Dialog Boxes

In this lesson, you'll learn how to select commands in menus and dialog boxes.

Menu Basics

A menu presents you with a list of commands. When you open a menu, you can select a command, and OS/2 will perform that command for you. You'll find many different types of menus in OS/2:

- A **pop-up menu** (see Figure 7.1) appears when you right-click on an object. From this menu, you can copy, move, open the object, or change its settings.

Figure 7.1 A pop-up menu appears when you right-click on an object.

- A **menu bar** appears along the top of most program windows (see Figure 7.2). Click on one of the menu names, and a drop-down menu appears, revealing a list of commands.

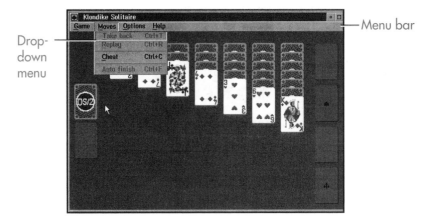

Figure 7.2   Most programs contain menu bars.

- Every window has a special **window menu**, which appears when you click once on the title-bar icon (see Figure 7.3). The commands on the window menu arrange icons in the window, close the window, move, resize, or hide the window, and change the window settings.

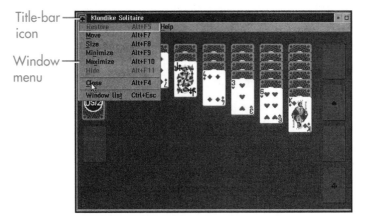

Figure 7.3   Here's the special window menu.

Selecting a Menu Command

When working with any menu, remember these tips:

The selected command is highlighted.

Because this command appears gray, you can't select it now.

Press the underlined letter to select the command once the menu is open.

Press these shortcut keys to select this command without opening the menu.

These three dots mean this command will display a dialog box when selected.

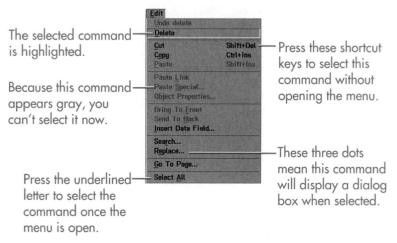

Figure 7.4 A typical menu.

- To open a menu, click on it.

- To select a menu command, click on it. (The selected command is highlighted.)

- If a command appears gray, it is currently unavailable; you cannot select it.

- If you select a command followed by an ellipsis (three dots), a dialog box will appear. You'll learn how to select options in a dialog box later in this chapter.

> **Dialog Box** A special box that appears when the program needs more information from you in order to execute a command.

- A check mark in front of a command indicates that the option is turned on. Select the command again to turn the option off (remove the check mark).

- A right-pointing arrow to the right of a command indicates that when you select the command, a cascading menu will appear. Just slide your mouse over to this menu and select your command.

- A right-pointing arrow *button* to the right of a command indicates that the command has some kind of default option. To select the command itself, just click on it. To change the default option, click on the arrow button to open the cascading menu, and then select the option you want (see Figure 7.5).

To sort the icons in a folder, click on the Sort command.

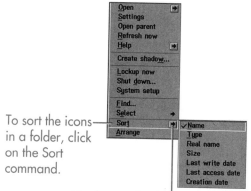

To change the Sort option, click on the arrow button to display the cascading menu.

Figure 7.5 Change the options for a command on the cascading menu.

- Without opening a menu, you can select a command by pressing its *shortcut keys* on the keyboard. (The shortcut keys appear to the right of the command name on the menu.) Not every command has a shortcut key assigned to it. For example, if you look back at Figure 7.4, you'll see that the shortcut key Shift+Del is assigned to the Cut command. You can press Shift+Del to cut text *without* opening a menu.

- If you open a menu by mistake, click somewhere outside the menu to close it again. You can also close a menu by pressing Esc.

The Parts of a Dialog Box

When you select a menu command followed by an ellipsis, a dialog box appears. This is the program's way of asking you for the information it needs to carry out the command. Figure 7.6 contains some common dialog box components:

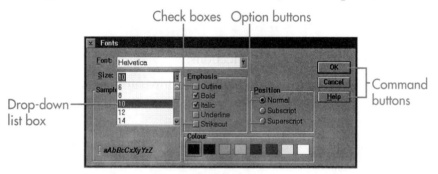

Figure 7.6 A typical dialog box.

List box Presents a list of items, such as a list of files, to choose from. In order to use a drop-down list box, you must open it first by clicking on the arrow to the side of the box.

Text box Provides a place for you to type information, such as the name of a file.

Check boxes Represent options that can be turned on or off. A check mark indicates that the option is on. (Note the Bold and Italic check boxes in Figure 7.6.)

Option buttons   Like check boxes, these represent options you can turn on or off. However, option buttons appear as a group, and they are mutually exclusive, which means you can only pick one. (Note the Normal, Subscript, and Superscript options buttons in Figure 7.6.) When an option button is selected, a dot appears inside it.

Command buttons   Perform some command. For example, OK closes the dialog box and uses your selections to carry out the command, and Cancel closes the dialog box without performing the command at all. Help takes you to the Help section for that dialog box.

Making Choices in a Dialog Box

To make your dialog box selections:

- In a list box, click on the up or down arrows of the scroll bar to scroll through the items in the list. Then click on an item to select it.

- To open a drop-down list box, click on the arrow to the right of the box. Then click on an item to select it.

- To select an option button or check box, click on it to toggle the option on or off. Remember that option buttons are mutually exclusive; selecting one "deselects" the others.

- In a text box, you simply type whatever value you want. If you want to delete what's already there, drag over it to highlight it, and then type your data. What you type replaces what was in the box.

- To close the dialog box and carry out the command with the selections you've indicated, click on OK.

- To exit a dialog box without completing the command, click on Cancel or press Esc.

The Settings Notebook

You use the Settings notebook to change the settings for a particular object (for example, to change the icon associated with that object). To display the Settings notebook for an object, right-click on the object and select Settings from the pop-up menu. For example, to display the Settings notebook for the Desktop (shown in Figure 7.7), right-click on the Desktop and then select Settings.

Double-click on the title-bar icon to close the notebook.

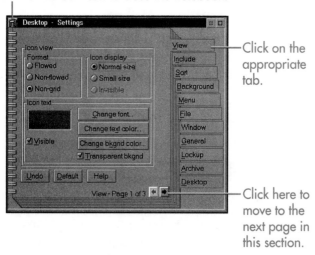

Click on the appropriate tab.

Click here to move to the next page in this section.

Figure 7.7   The Settings notebook for the Desktop.

The Settings notebook is really just a series of dialog boxes separated by tabs. Inside, you'll find all the usual dialog box components: list boxes, drop-down lists, check boxes, option buttons, command buttons, and text boxes. Making your selections in the Settings notebook is the same as it is inside any other dialog box.

Follow these guidelines to move about within the Settings notebook.

- To move from section to section in the Settings notebook, click on the appropriate tab.

- To move from page to page within a section, click on the left or right arrows at the bottom of each page.

- To close the Settings notebook, double-click on the title-bar icon. This is the same as clicking on OK in an ordinary dialog box. Although there is no Cancel button in the Settings notebook, there are lots of Default and Undo buttons you can use to reset your changes to what they were.

Different types of objects use different types of settings, so each Settings notebook may look a bit different. Although you will rarely want to change an object's settings, here are some things you might want to try:

- To change the icon for an object, click on the General tab, and then click on Edit (to make changes to the icon) or Create another (to create another icon).

- To have OS/2 display the minimized window as an icon at the bottom of the screen instead of placing it in the Minimized Window Viewer, click on the Window tab and select Minimize window to desktop.

- If you want to turn a data-file into a template so you can reuse it, create a data-file, and then click on the General tab and select the Template option.

- To change the way objects are arranged within a folder, use the options on the Sort tab.

- To change the size of icons in a folder, use the options on the View tab.

- To change the color of a folder's window, use the options on the Background tab. You can also use it to put a picture (called a bitmap) in the background of a folder instead of just plain color. (Also, since the Desktop is a folder, you can change the color of the desktop or add a bitmap as well.)

> **Add a Bitmap to a Folder Window?**   Although you can do this, it is different from Windows, which only lets you add a bitmap to the desktop. Also, in Windows, you change the color of *all windows*—not individual ones. In OS/2 Warp, you can customize each folder window as well as the Desktop.

In this lesson, you learned how to select menu commands and make choices in dialog boxes. In the next lesson, you'll learn the basics of working with objects.

Lesson

Working with Objects

In this lesson, you'll learn how to open, close, select, and arrange objects.

Opening and Closing Objects

To use most objects, you must first open them. To open an object, simply double-click on it, and a window appears. To close the window later on, double-click on its title-bar icon.

When an object is open, OS/2 displays little hash marks behind it to remind you that it's still open somewhere. In the case of a folder object, the folder icon itself changes to look like it's open (see Figure 8.1). Therefore, if an object is open but its window is not visible, you know that the window is minimized or hidden and you can find it in the Window list (see Lesson 6).

Figure 8.1 An open folder icon looks like this.

What happens when you double-click on (or open) an object depends on what type of object it is.

- When you open a folder object, it opens out into a window, displaying all the objects stored in the folder.

- When you open a program object, you start the program.

- When you open a data-file object, you start the application in which the data-file was created and tell it to load the data-file for you. For example, if you double-click on a data-file called Letter Home, your word processing program starts and opens your letter (which is all ready for you to add your changes).

- When you open a device object, a window opens to display information about what the device is currently doing. For example, if you double-click on the Printer device object, you can see which files are in line to print.

To later close the object, double-click on its title-bar icon.

Selecting an Object

To do something with an object (such as copy, move, delete, open, or change its settings), you must select it first. To select an object, just click on it. The selected object appears gray to let you know it's "chosen."

Wrong One   If you choose the wrong object by mistake, click anywhere on the Desktop to deselect the object or just click on another object to select it instead.

You can select multiple objects and perform the same task with all of them at once. For example, if you want to delete a group of files, you can select several data-file objects and then delete them in one step.

To select multiple objects that are located together (contiguous), follow these steps:

1. Click at the upper left-hand corner of the group with the left mouse button.

2. Still holding down the mouse button, drag downward and to the right to draw a lasso around the objects you want to select.

3. Release the mouse button. The surrounded objects appear gray, which means they're selected (see Figure 8.2).

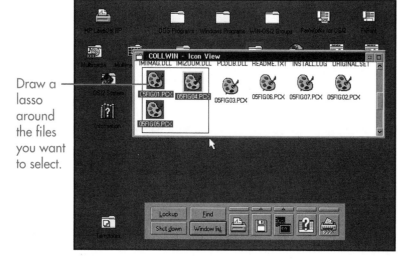

Draw a lasso around the files you want to select.

Figure 8.2 Selecting multiple files.

Quick Select To quickly select objects that are located together, just drag the mouse pointer over them.

To select multiple objects that are not grouped together (non-contiguous), follow these steps:

1. Use the lasso technique to select as many objects as you can.

2. Press and hold the Ctrl key as you click on the extra objects you want to select. (Your original ones will remain selected.)

3. To deselect any object you don't want within a
   group, press and hold the Ctrl key and click on the
   selected object to deselect it.

> **Select Everything!** If you want to select all
> the objects in a window, just right-click inside the
> window and choose Select from the pop-up
> menu. Then click on Select all.

> **Another Way** You can also press Ctrl+/
> (the Ctrl key and the forward slash key) to
> select all the objects in a window, which is
> exactly what you would do in Windows' File
> Manager to select all the files in a directory.

Dragging and Dropping an Object

Drag-and-drop is exactly what it sounds like: dragging one
object to another object and dropping it (letting go of the
right mouse button). You drag and drop to get one object to
do something with another. For example, you can drag and
drop a data-file object onto the Printer object to print the
file. You can drag and drop one object or a group of objects.
Here's how to use drag-and-drop:

1. Select the object(s) you want to drag and drop.

2. Point to the selected group, and press and hold the
   right mouse button.

3. Drag the object(s) over another object and release
   the mouse button.

> **I Didn't Want to Do That** If you change
> your mind while doing a drag-and-drop, press
> Esc to cancel the action.

This Seems Different   If you're used to Windows, dragging is different in OS/2. In Windows, you drag with the left button; in OS/2, you drag with the right button.

You can drag and drop objects onto the Shredder to delete them or drag and drop objects onto the Printer object to print them. Likewise, you can drag and drop objects from one folder into another to move them or drag and drop objects onto the Drive A object to copy them to a diskette (see Figure 8.3).

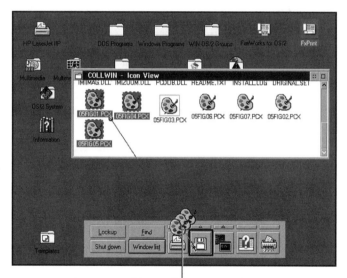

Drag your files to the Drive A object to copy them onto a diskette.

Figure 8.3   An example of drag-and-drop.

When you try to drag and drop an object onto something you shouldn't, OS/2 Warp displays a black circle with a vertical line through it to tell you that the action is not possible.

Pickup Versus Drag-and-Drop

You can "pick up" objects instead of dragging them. When you pick up an object, you can perform some additional operations on the object—such as opening the folder you want to drop the object into—before you drop it.

To use the pickup feature, follow these steps:

1. Select the objects you want to pick up.

2. Press Alt and then right-click on the objects.

3. Select Pickup.

4. Do what you want to your selected group. Then drag the objects to their destination and drop them.

If you want to cancel a pickup, click on your selected objects with the right mouse button and select Cancel drag.

Arranging Objects

When the objects on the Desktop or within one of your folders get out of line, you can easily arrange them by following these simple steps:

1. Right-click on the Desktop or right-click within a folder.

2. From the pop-up menu, select Arrange.

> **But I Don't Like It!**   If you don't like your new arrangement, repeat these steps and choose Undo arrange. Objects are arranged based on the settings you'll find under the View tab of the Settings notebook.

In this lesson, you learned how to open, close, and select objects, among other things. In the next lesson, you'll learn how to copy, move, rename, and delete objects.

Lesson

9

Copying, Moving, Deleting, and Renaming Objects

In this lesson, you'll learn how to copy, move, delete, and rename your objects.

Copying and Shadowing Objects

There are two ways to copy an object: a simple, straightforward *copy* and a *shadow*.

A copy creates a duplicate of the original object. If you later change the original object somehow, the copy does not change. Each object represents a distinctly different file on the hard disk.

A shadow is just another object or icon that remains linked to the original file. Suppose, for example, you make a shadow of an object, and then open the original object and edit the file. When you access the object through the shadow icon later, you'll see the same changes you made to the original object because both icons (objects) are linked to the same solitary file on the hard disk. A shadow object is easy to spot: it has a blue title.

So Why Create a Shadow? A shadow provides easy access to the same file from lots of different places. For example, you can add shadows to the LaunchPad to provide easy access to such commonly used objects as your word processor or your day planner. If you made copies instead, your hard disk would be cluttered with unnecessary extra files. Create a copy only when you want to save a duplicate of important data.

Copying Objects

Follow these steps to make a copy of an object:

1. Press and hold the Ctrl key.

2. Click on the object with the right mouse button and drag the copy to its new location.

3. Release the mouse button. You'll be asked whether you want to rename the copy so you can tell it apart from the original. (If you drag the copy to a different folder, you can leave the name the same as the original if you want.)

4. If you want to rename the copy, type in a new name and click on OK. If you're copying something over an older version of itself, you may want to select Replace existing object instead.

You can copy multiple objects at once if you want. Just select them first, and then Ctrl+drag the entire group to its new location. For example, you could copy multiple files onto a diskette by selecting them, pressing Ctrl, and dragging them as a group to the Drive A object.

Why Can't I Make a Copy?   Some objects (such as the Shredder, the Drive C object, and the Printer) can't be copied, they can only be shadowed. If you try to copy them, you'll just end up with a shadow instead (which links the icon to the same part of the computer that the original icon does).

Gentle Reminder   Remember to press Ctrl when copying; if you don't, OS/2 assumes you're moving the objects instead. However, if you're copying files to a *different* drive, you don't need to press the Ctrl key.

Shadowing Objects

Follow these steps to make a shadow of an object:

1. Press and hold Ctrl+Shift.

2. Right-click on the object you want to shadow and drag the object to its new location. (As you drag, you'll see a line stretching out between the original object and the shadow.)

3. Release the mouse button. You won't be asked whether you want to rename the shadow copy. Because the shadow is linked to the original, if you change the name of the shadow object, the original is changed (and vice versa).

If you delete a shadow, the original object remains intact. However, if you delete the original object, all shadows are deleted as well.

If you want to find the original object that a shadow is linked to, right-click on the shadow, select Original from the pop-up menu, and select Locate. You'll be escorted to the location of the original.

The Create Another Option

OS/2 Warp has an option called Create another that's similar to copying. It creates an empty copy of the object, just the way a *template* does (see Lesson 17), but Create another saves you the trouble of going all the way back to the Templates folder to create something like a new folder or a new spreadsheet. To use the Create another option, follow these steps:

1. Right-click on the object you want to use as a template for some new object.

2. From the menu that appears, select Create another.

For example, right-click on an existing spreadsheet object, select Create another, and create a new blank spreadsheet instead of a copy of the original.

> **Templates**   A template is like a form you fill in to create a new object that's very similar to the template object. You can use a template to create a new folder, a new letter, or a new spreadsheet, for example.

Moving Objects

You can move objects wherever you like; for example, you might want to move objects from one folder into another to make them easier to locate. To move an object, follow these steps:

1. Click on the object with the right mouse button.

2. Drag the object to its new location.

3. Release the mouse button.

Gentle Reminder If you're moving objects to a different drive, you have to press Shift and then drag. If you don't, OS/2 thinks you're trying to copy the objects instead.

You can move multiple objects at once if you want. Just select them and drag the entire group to its new location. For example, you could move multiple objects from one folder to another by selecting them and dragging them as a group to the new folder. (By the way, moving objects from one folder to another is the same as moving them from one directory to another on the hard disk.)

I Didn't Want to Move That! Normally, when you move or copy an object, Warp simply carries out that act without asking for confirmation. If you'd like to confirm your move or copy operations, you can change the system setup. Right-click on the Desktop and select System setup from the pop-up menu. Double-click on the System icon, click on the Confirmations tab, and select Confirm on copy, move, create shadow.

Harder Than Windows? In OS/2 Warp, you can't fine-tune the placement of your objects by moving them a short distance, the way you can in Windows. If you try, you'll see the No-you-can't-do-that symbol. Instead, move the object farther away, and then move it back.

If you're just trying to arrange things neatly, use the Arrange command instead of moving icons one by one. But be careful: the result is not the same as with Windows, where the icons simply straighten themselves out. In OS/2, the icons are arranged in a particular order depending on how you have that window set up. Refer to Lesson 6.

Deleting Objects

When you delete an object, you usually delete the actual
file it refers to. One exception to this is when you delete
a shadow object, which deletes only the shadow, not the
original file or the original object.

Deleting a folder removes the folder and everything in
it, so be sure you don't need anything in it before you delete
a folder. Deleting a program object, on the other hand, deletes only the program's start button (the icon), and not all
the files that make the program go. If you accidentally delete
a program icon, you can easily get OS/2 to recreate it; see
Lesson 25.

Follow these steps to delete an object:

1. Right-click on the object.

2. Drag the object to the Shredder (located on the
   LaunchPad). You'll see the warning shown in
   Figure 9.1.

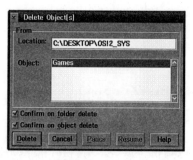

Figure 9.1 You'll see a warning before any files are actually
deleted.

3. Click on Delete to finish the job.

4. If you have the Confirm on object delete option
   turned on, you'll see another confirmation box.
   Click on Yes to delete your object; click on Yes to

all to delete all the objects you selected; click on No to stop the deletion of this one object; click on Cancel if you've changed your mind about deleting the objects (Cancel returns you to OS/2); click on Pause to stop a mass deletion once it has started.

To delete multiple objects, select them and drag the group to the Shredder. You can also select an object and press Delete if dragging is not your style.

Renaming Objects

An object has two names: its *title*, which appears underneath the object on-screen, and its *file name*, which is the name of the file to which the object refers. A title can consist of any number of characters and can include spaces and periods. You can even have a two-line title if a long title is taking up too much room on-screen.

When you change an object's title, OS/2 uses as much of the title as it can to change the file name too. For example, the spaces in a title may be translated into an underscore (_) in the file name. You'll learn more about the file name limitations in Lesson 11.

To rename an object, follow these steps:

1. Press and hold the Alt key.

2. Click on the object.

3. Drag over the old title, and then type a new title. To continue the title on a second line, press Enter and type the rest of the title.

4. Click anywhere on the Desktop to save the new title.

In this lesson, you learned how to copy, move, delete, and rename objects. In the next lesson, you'll learn how to create and delete folders.

Lesson

Managing Folders

In this lesson, you'll learn how to create, delete, and manage your folders.

Creating a Folder

You create new *directories* on your hard disk by creating new folders. Folders are the visual representation of the directories on the hard disk. You can place anything you want in a folder: not just data files, but also program objects, device objects, and other folders.

> **Directory** Files are organized on the hard disk within directories, which are like the drawers of a large filing cabinet. By keeping files in different directories, you can locate and work with related files more easily.

Not all of the directories on your PC's hard disk appear as folders on the Desktop. Only the directories/folders that OS/2 thinks you'll use the most appear. When you add a new directory to the hard disk, you can add it to the Desktop, which makes it easier to access, or you can simply add it to the Drive C window (see Figure 10.1).

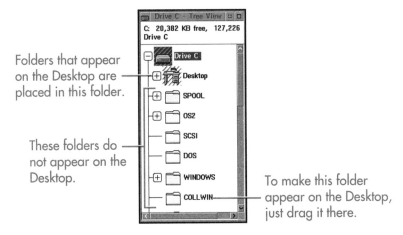

Folders that appear on the Desktop are placed in this folder.

These folders do not appear on the Desktop.

To make this folder appear on the Desktop, just drag it there.

Figure 10.1   The Drive C window.

Folders that appear on the Desktop are subdirectories or subfolders of the \DESKTOP directory. For example, I used a program called Collage for Windows to capture the screen shots for this book, so the screen shots were saved in the COLLWIN directory/folder. I wanted easy access to this directory/folder, so I opened the Drive C window and dragged the COLLWIN folder onto my Desktop. In the Drive C window, I saw OS/2 move the COLLWIN folder from its original location to the DESKTOP folder. On the Desktop, I saw the COLLWIN folder object appear, ready for me to use.

To create a new folder (directory), follow these steps:

1. Double-click on the Templates folder to open it.

2. Click on the Folder icon with the right mouse button and drag a template off the stack.

3. Drag the folder template onto the Desktop or into another folder (to create a folder within a folder, as shown in Figure 10.2). If you don't want the folder to appear on the Desktop, open the Drive C window and drag the folder template there. (For help in opening the Drive C window, see Lesson 13.)

Drag a folder template onto the Desktop or into another folder.

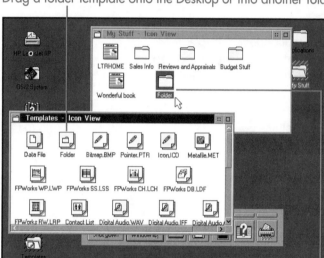

Then rename the folder.

Figure 10.2 Create a new folder with the Folder template.

4. Release the mouse button, and the folder appears.

5. To give the new folder a name, press and hold the Alt key and click on the folder. Drag over the existing name and type a new name. Click anywhere on the Desktop to save the name.

> **Another Way to Create a Folder** If you open a window on drive C, you can add a subdirectory (or a folder within a folder) by right-clicking on an existing folder. From the menu that appears, click on the arrow next to Create another and select Folder. In the box that appears, click on the Related tab, click on the folder/directory in which you want to place your new folder, and then click on Create. You'll still need to give your folder a real name (it's simply called Folder by default) by pressing Alt and selecting it.

Adding Objects to a Folder

Once you've created a folder, you can add objects to that folder by simply dragging them there. You can drag data-files, program icons, or whatever.

1. Right-click on the object you want to add to the folder.

2. Drag the object to the folder and release the mouse button.

Save Time   A folder does not have to be open for you to drag something into it. When you drag an icon on top of a closed folder, a red square appears around the folder to tell you that you've hit the "mark." Let go, and your object is placed inside the folder.

Saving Data-Files to a Folder

When you save a file within a program such as a word processor, the program asks you to name that file and indicate where (in which folder or directory) you want to store it. Type a name for your file, and then under Directory, double-click on the folder to which you want to save your data-file (see Figure 10.3). Click on Save, and OS/2 saves your file to the folder you selected. (For more help on saving a file, see Lesson 17.)

Type a file name here.

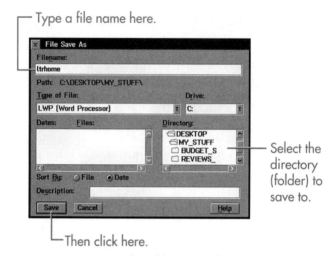

Select the directory (folder) to save to.

Then click here.

Figure 10.3   Save your data-file in your favorite folder.

Renaming a Folder

If a folder's name no longer describes its contents, it's time to change the name of that folder. To rename a folder:

1. Press and hold the Alt key and click on the folder.

2. Drag over the existing name and type a new name. If the name for the folder is long, you can type part of the name on a second line by pressing Enter and then typing the rest of the name.

3. Click anywhere on the Desktop to save the name.

Deleting a Folder

When you delete a folder, all the objects in that folder are also deleted. Although you can undelete objects if you act immediately after accidentally deleting them, undeleting those objects becomes more difficult if you delete the folder they were in. So be careful when choosing a folder to delete.

To delete a folder:

1. Right-click on the folder.

2. Drag the folder to the Shredder on the LaunchPad.

3. Release the mouse button.

4. Click on Delete to confirm the deletion.

5. If you selected Confirm on object delete in the previous dialog box, you'll see another warning. Click on Yes to continue or No to stop the deletion. If you selected several objects for deletion, you can delete them all by clicking on Yes to all. Click on Cancel to stop the deletion process.

Fast Deletion   You can also delete a folder by clicking on it and pressing Delete.

Locating a Lost Folder or File

Large hard disks tend to collect a large number of files, making it difficult to find one particular folder or file. With the Find command, you can locate a lost folder, file, or other object.

1. Click on the Find button on the LaunchPad. The Find Objects dialog box appears, as shown in Figure 10.4.

Check this box if you want to save the location of the object.

Type the name of the object to search for here.

Figure 10.4   Searching for a lost file.

2. Type the name of the object you want to search for (Find looks at the title of an object to find a match.)

> **What If I Don't Know the Exact Name?**   Just type what you're sure of and use an asterisk (*) to represent any unknown characters. For example, type * **sales** * to find your First Quarter Sales Chart and Second Quarter Sales Chart objects.

3. Click on Find. A Find Results window opens, and there's a shadow copy of your object. Do what you will with the shadow; it doesn't affect the original object.

4. Click on Close when you're done with this window (or Return if you need to try the Find process again).

Searching for Text Inside a File

If you don't know the name of the file you're looking for, but you know it contains a specific phrase (such as "the Benham project"), you can have OS/2 search *inside* files for your missing file. To do so, follow these steps:

1. Double-click on the OS/2 System folder to open it. Open the Productivity folder.

2. Double-click on the Seek and Scan Files icon. You'll see a window like the one shown in Figure 10.5.

Type the name(s) of the files to search for.

These two files meet the search criteria.

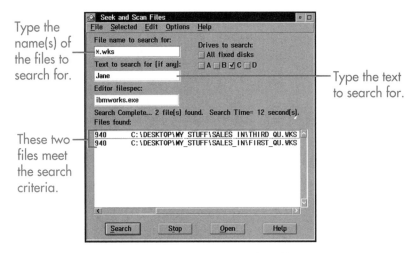

Type the text to search for.

Figure 10.5 Searching for text inside a file.

3. Type a file name to look for or use wild cards to search for several similar files. For example, if you know the file was created in your word processor and all those files end in .DOC, type *.DOC in the File name to search for box. If you don't remember the name, but you think it starts with a W, type W*.DOC instead.

4. Type the text you want to search for in the Text to search for box. For example, type Benham project.

5. Click on Search. Warp searches the files you specified, looking for the text you typed. When it finds a match, it places the file name in the Files found box, but continues to search every file specified. You can stop it midway by clicking on Stop if you want.

In this lesson, you learned how to create and delete folders and how to locate lost files and folders. In the next lesson, you'll learn how to name and rename files.

Lesson

Naming and Renaming Files

In this lesson, you'll learn how to name and rename files.

Naming Files

When you create a file, such as a letter, a chart, or a spreadsheet, you must give that file a name. Most files have a first and a last name separated by a period. The last name of a file generally identifies what type of file it is. For example, program files usually end in .EXE. A document file might have the last name .DOC, and a spreadsheet file might end in .WK4, .XLS, or, as in the case of IBM Works, .LSS.

What type of name you can give a file actually depends on the type of file system you're using. If you're using the FAT file system (you are if you installed OS/2 using the Easy option), a file name must be no more than eight characters, followed by an optional period and an extension of up to three characters (as in MADSTONE.XLS).

> **FAT File System**   The file handling system used by DOS. If you were already using DOS when you installed OS/2 Warp, you did not have to replace the FAT system. The FAT system imposes file name limitations.

HPFS File System The file handling system used by OS/2 Warp. HPFS is more efficient than the FAT file system, and it allows longer file names. You do not have to use HPFS to use OS/2 Warp; you can use FAT if you prefer.

If you're using the HPFS file system that comes with OS/2 (you might have installed this if you used the Advanced installation option), a file name can contain as many as 254 characters and as many periods as you like. For example, you could name a file the following:

COMPARISON.OF.MADISON.PROJECT.TO.STONES.PROJECT

How Can I Be Sure? To find out which file system you're using, right-click on the Drive C object and select Settings. Click on the Details tab and select File System Type.

Whether you're naming a file under FAT or HPFS, you can't use the following characters:

" / \ : * ? ¦ < > - &

Keep these additional rules in mind when naming files:

- With HPFS, a file can contain up to 254 characters (which includes the optional extension).

- A FAT file name can contain only eight characters, followed by an optional extension of up to three characters. The file name and the extension must be separated by a period.

- An HPFS file name can include any number of spaces or periods.

- A FAT file name can include only one period, which is used to separate the file name from the extension.

A FAT file name can not include any spaces at all; however, you can use underscores (_) instead of spaces if you want (as in 95_SALES.XLS).

Not the Same Name   You can't place two objects with the exact same name in the same folder (directory).

Generally, you name a file the first time you save it (see Figure 11.1). Most programs add the proper extension for you, so you don't have to worry about that. For more details on saving files, see Lesson 17.

Type a file name here.

Most programs add their own extensions (such as .LWP) to your file name.

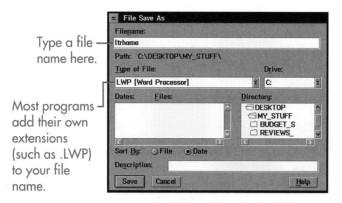

Figure 11.1   You name a file the first time you save it.

Renaming a File

When you change the *title* of an object (the thing that appears under the object on-screen), Warp changes the file name associated with that object. Although you can use spaces in a title, you can't always use them in a file name; the rules for naming files are more restrictive (see the previous section). When converting the title into a file name, Warp takes these restrictions into account. For example, if you use the FAT file system and you change the title of an object to

EE Calendar.WKS, Warp changes the file name to
EE_CALEN.WKS because a FAT file name can't include
spaces.

To rename a file, you change its title as described here:

1. Press and hold the Alt key and click on the data-file
   object.

2. Drag over the existing name and type a new name.
   (See the previous section for file name restrictions.)

3. Click anywhere on the Desktop to save the name.
   Warp converts the new title into a new valid file
   name.

In this lesson, you learned how to name and rename
files. In the next lesson, you'll learn how to copy, move,
delete, and undelete files.

Lesson 12

Copying, Moving, and Deleting Files

In this lesson, you'll learn how to copy, move, delete, and undelete files.

Copying and Moving Files

You copy or move a file just as you would any other object (see Lesson 9). If the file is located in a folder that is visible on the Desktop, open the folder first by double-clicking on it. If the file's folder is not visible on the Desktop, you'll have to open a drive window to see the file.

> **Make It Easy** Put the folders you need on the Desktop so they'll be easier to access. Remember, not all directories are visible as folders on your Desktop. To move a directory (folder) to the Desktop, drag it from the Drive C window out onto the Desktop. Be careful about moving directories that a program expects to find in a particular place. If you're not sure whether it's safe to move a particular directory/folder onto the Desktop, create your own folder and drag your data-files into it. See Lesson 10.

To open a Drive C window, click on the LaunchPad drawer handle, and then click on the Drive C button (see Figure 12.1). To open a Drive A window, click on the Drive A button on the LaunchPad. (Make sure you first insert a diskette into drive A.) You'll learn more about drive windows in Lesson 13.

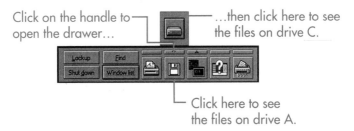

Click on the handle to open the drawer...

...then click here to see the files on drive C.

Click here to see the files on drive A.

Figure 12.1   Open a drive window if necessary before you copy or move a file.

You can copy or move files between a drive window and another drive window or between a drive window and a folder on the Desktop. Just open the appropriate drive window and folders and position them so that they are completely visible before you attempt to copy or move a file.

- To *copy* a file, press Ctrl and drag the file to another location. You don't need to press the Ctrl key if you're copying files from one drive (such as your hard disk) to another (such as a diskette).

- To *move* a file, press Shift and drag the file to its new home. You don't need to press the Shift key if you're moving files from one directory (folder) to another directory (folder) on the same drive or if you're moving a file object from one folder to another on the Desktop.

Just Like File Manager   OS/2's method of copying and moving files (especially the use of the Shift and Ctrl keys) is similar to Windows. So you should feel right at home.

You can copy or move multiple files at once by select-ing a group of them first. Use one of these three methods to select your files:

- Press the right mouse button and drag over the files you want to select.

- If you need to select files that aren't next to each other, press and hold the Ctrl key, and then click on the files one by one.

- You can also lasso the files you want by clicking at the upper left-hand corner of your group and drag-ging down to the right-hand corner, as shown in Figure 12.2.

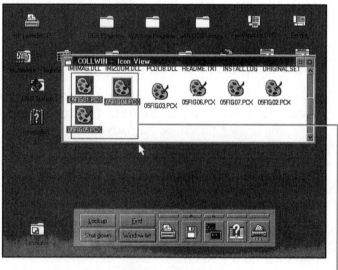

Draw a lasso around the files you want to select. ⎯

Figure 12.2 Selecting a group of files.

If You Use HPFS... Although Warp can deal with files created using either the FAT or the HPFS file system, DOS can read only those files saved using the FAT filing system. However, even if you are using HPFS, you can share your files with DOS users; when you copy files to a diskette, Warp automatically adjusts the file name to fit the eight-plus-three FAT limitation. Just be sure to use the drag-and-drop method of copying files (not the actual COPY command that you might type at a command prompt).

Deleting Files

You also delete a file just as you would any other object (see Lesson 9). If the file is located in a folder that is visible on the Desktop, open the folder first by double-clicking on it. Otherwise, you'll have to open a drive window to see it. Just be sure to open the drive window in Icon view or Detail view, both of which display the files on that drive. (As you'll learn in Lesson 13, Tree view does not list files; it lists only directories or folders.)

Once the file is visible, delete it in one of two ways:

- Click on the file with the right mouse button and drag it to the Shredder (located on the LaunchPad).

- Click on the file and press Delete.

You can delete multiple files by selecting them first. See the previous section for tips on how to select files.

Undeleting a File

It's inevitable. At some point in your computing lifetime, you will accidentally delete a file you need. When that time comes, don't panic. With the UNDELETE command, you might be able to retrieve the deleted file. If you have OS/2 set up to track your deleted files (see the next section) and you act immediately, there's a good chance you can save the file. If you don't meet both of those criteria, you probably won't be successful—but it's still worth a try.

Follow these steps to use the UNDELETE command to retrieve a deleted file:

1. Click on the OS/2 Prompt button, located on the LaunchPad (see Figure 12.3). A window opens and displays the OS/2 prompt, **[C:\]**. (Command prompts are discussed in more detail in Lesson 19.)

OS/2 prompt window

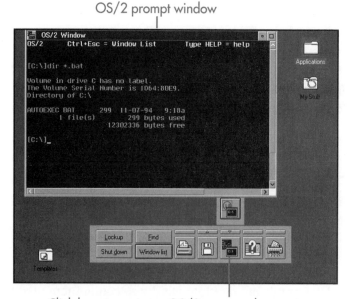

Click here to go to an OS/2 command prompt.

Figure 12.3   Using the OS/2 command prompt.

2. At the prompt, type UNDELETE /S.

3. Press Enter.

4. Warp checks for recently deleted files and produces a list. If you see your file, press Y to undelete it. Press N to bypass a file.

5. To return to OS/2, type **EXIT** and press Enter. Your file shows up exactly where it was, in whatever folder you deleted it from.

> **Oh, Well...** If you see the message **DIRCMD environment variable not present**, the UNDELETE feature is not turned on, so Warp can't help you get your file back. See the section "Setting Up the UNDELETE Feature" for help. In the meantime, if you have DOS version 5 or higher, you might still have a chance to get your file back; read the section, "Undeleting a File with DOS."

Setting Up the UNDELETE Feature

For the OS/2 Warp UNDELETE feature to work, it must be enabled. Enabling it involves editing one of the PC's configuration files, the CONFIG.SYS.

> **What About My Old Files?** Turning on the UNDELETE feature will not enable you to retrieve previously deleted files. See the next section for ways in which DOS might be able to help you.

1. Double-click on the OS/2 System folder to open it. Then open the Productivity folder.

2. Double-click on the OS/2 System Editor icon.

3. Click on the File menu and select Open. Under Open filename, type **C:\CONFIG.SYS**. Click on Open.

4. Use the down arrow key or the scroll bars to locate the line that reads **REM SET DELDIR=C:\DELETE,512;**. (If it doesn't look exactly like that, that's okay; it'll vary depending on how your PC is set up.)

5. Use the arrow keys to move the cursor under the R in REM, and then press Delete four times to delete the word REM and the space that follows it. The line should now read **SET DELDIR=C:\DELETE,512;**.

6. Save the file by opening the File menu and clicking on Save.

7. Exit the editor by double-clicking on the title-bar icon.

8. Exit OS/2 by clicking on the Shut down button on the LaunchPad. Restart your PC so the changes take effect and the UNDELETE feature is turned on. From now on, UNDELETE will be activated automatically whenever you start your PC.

Undeleting a File with DOS

For OS/2 to recover a file, its UNDELETE tracking system must be turned on. However, if your PC uses DOS 5 or higher and you installed Dual Boot (which you did if you installed OS/2 using the Easy method), you may still have a chance to recover your file.

1. Double-click on the OS/2 System folder to open it. Then open the Command Prompts folder.

2. Double-click on the Dual Boot icon. Press Y and Enter, and your PC will restart. You'll see a DOS prompt, **C:\>**.

3. Change to the directory in which you lost your file. For example, if you deleted a file out of the MY STUFF folder, type **CD\MY_STUFF** and press Enter.

4. Type **UNDELETE** and press Enter again.

5. DOS displays a list of recently deleted files. To recover a file, press Y. Press N to bypass a file.

6. If you select a file to recover, DOS needs you to supply the first letter of your file. Type that letter and press Enter.

7. To return to OS/2, type **C:\OS2\BOOT /OS2** and press Enter. You'll see a window asking you whether you want to start DOS again.

8. Click on the window to activate it. Then press N and Enter.

In this lesson, you learned how to copy, move, delete, and undelete your files. In the next lesson, you'll learn how to list the files on a disk and how to format or copy a diskette.

Lesson 13

Managing Your Disks

In this lesson, you'll learn how to list the files on a disk, format a diskette, and copy a diskette.

Listing the Files on a Disk or a Diskette

To find out what's on a disk, you open up its device object (icon). Figure 13.1 shows the icons for Drive C and Drive A.

Click here to open the drawer...

... then click here to list the files on Drive C.

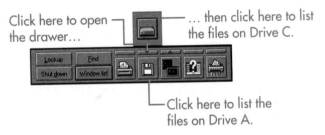

Click here to list the files on Drive A.

Figure 13.1   To list the files on a disk, open its device object.

- To list the files on your hard disk (Drive C), click on the drawer handle on the LaunchPad to open it. Then click on the Drive C object. (See Figure 13.1.)

- To list the files on a diskette in Drive A, insert the diskette, and then click once on the Drive A object on the LaunchPad.

What About My Other Drives?   You'll find device objects for your other drives (such as Drive B) in the Drives folder. To get to it, open the OS/2 System folder, and then open the Drives folder. Double-click on a drive icon to open its window.

When you click on a drive's device object, a window appears. Figure 13.2 shows the two drive windows you'd see if you followed the instructions in both bulleted items above.

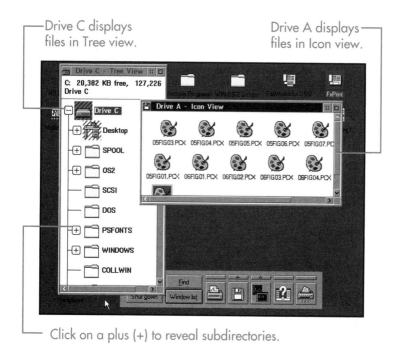

─Drive C displays files in Tree view.

Drive A displays─ files in Icon view.

── Click on a plus (+) to reveal subdirectories.

Figure 13.2   Finding out what files you have on disk.

By default, Drive C displays its contents in Tree view, which shows you the hierarchy of folders (directories) on the drive. It also tells you how much room is left on a disk. Click on a plus sign (+) to reveal hidden folders (subdirectories). Click on a minus sign (−) to collapse subdirectories back into the parent directory. Tree view does not list the actual files on a disk; it lists only the directories (folders).

Drive A normally displays its contents in Icon view, where each file is represented by an icon. You may see folders here too; they represent directories on the diskette (if there are any). If you double-click on a folder in Icon view, you'll open another window that contains icons for the objects in that folder.

> **This Isn't Current** If you delete, copy, or move files in a window, that window will no longer be current. You can refresh the window by right-clicking on it and selecting the Refresh now command from the pop-up menu.

Changing the View

You can't change the view of an existing window. Instead, you have to open another window with the view you want. For this reason, it's best to select the view you want *before* you open a drive window instead of simply clicking on the drive object and getting the default view. Here's how to select a view as you open a window:

1. Right-click on the device object. For example, right-click on the Drive C button on the LaunchPad.

2. Click on the arrow to the right of the Open command.

3. Select the view you want to use. A window opens in that view listing the objects on the selected drive.

Tree view doesn't list files on a disk, and Icon view may take up too much room because it displays each file as an icon. Detail view is a nice compromise, as Figure 13.3 shows.

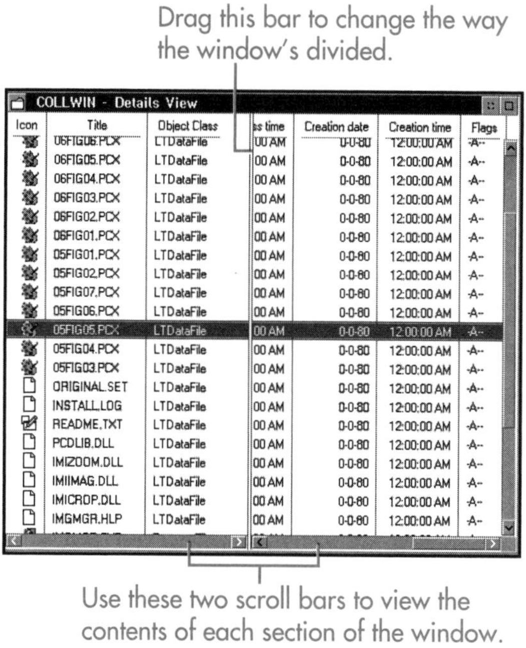

Drag this bar to change the way
the window's divided.

Use these two scroll bars to view the
contents of each section of the window.

Figure 13.3 Detail view.

Detail view lists the details about each file, including
the real name (file name), the object's title, the size, the date
and time of the last write (for example, when the file was
last changed by someone), and the date and time the file was
originally created, among other things. Detail view is divided
into two sections. Use the scroll bars at the bottom of each
section to view the hidden columns. For example, I've
already scrolled past some information in the second panel
in Figure 13.3. Click on the left scroll arrow to scroll back-
ward, so you can view some of the hidden information such
as the real name, size, and last write date. You can also drag
the divider bar to view more information in either panel.

Change the Sort   By default, files are sorted in the drive window by name. You can change the way the files are listed by right-clicking on the window and selecting the arrow to the right of the Sort command from the pop-up menu. Then select the type of sort you want.

Formatting a Diskette

Before you can use a diskette for the first time, you must prepare it for use via a process called *formatting*. A diskette only needs to be formatted once; if you purchase preformatted diskettes, you do not need to format them yourself.

Formatting Erases Data!   When you format a diskette, it erases all the data on that diskette. So do not reformat a previously used diskette unless you're sure you do not need the files it contains.

To format a diskette, follow these steps:

1. Place the diskette in the drive.

2. Right-click on the corresponding device object. For example, click with the right mouse button on the Drive A object.

3. Click on Format disk. The Format Disk dialog box appears, as shown in Figure 13.4.

4. If you want, type in a diskette name.

5. If you need to, change the setting in the Capacity box. (You must choose the correct capacity for the type of diskette you're formatting; if you're unsure, check the box the diskette came in.)

Type a name for
your diskette here.

Select the type of diskette
you want to format.

Figure 13.4   The Format Disk dialog box.

Capacity   The capacity of a diskette is
determined by its size and density. The density of
a diskette determines the amount of data it can
hold. For example, a high density 3.5-inch
diskette can hold 1.44 megabytes of data.

6. Click on Format.

7. When the diskette is formatted, you'll see a box
telling you the amount of usable space on the
diskette. Click on OK.

Why Does It Say "Bad Sectors?"   Bad
sectors might indicate bad spots on a diskette or,
more likely, that the diskette was formatted to the
wrong capacity. Check the diskette's box for the
correct information and try reformatting the diskette.

8. The Format Disk dialog box remains on-screen so
you can format more diskettes. If you do want to
format other disks, slip in another diskette and click
on Format to start the process all over again. Otherwise, click on Cancel to remove the dialog box.

Creating Emergency Diskettes

You never know when trouble's going to hit, but you can be
darn sure you don't want to be caught unprepared. So create
emergency diskettes. With these diskettes, you'll be able to
reboot your computer when it isn't working properly, check
the hard disk for problems, and even back up and restore
important files (see Lesson 14).

You'll need three high-density 3.5-inch diskettes to
create your set of emergency diskettes. Once you have those,
follow these steps, which walk you through the process.

1. Open up the OS/2 System folder, and then open the
System Setup folder.

2. Double-click on the Create Utility Diskettes icon.

3. Select A for Drive A and click on Create. Insert each
of the diskettes when asked. When you're done,
label your emergency diskettes and put them in a
very safe place.

Copying a Diskette

When you copy a diskette, you make an exact duplicate.
You'll often use this procedure when you buy a new program. For example, before installing a new program, you
should make exact copies of each of the installation diskettes. Then, if one of the original diskettes ever becomes
damaged, you still have a good set.

To make a copy of a diskette, get another diskette that's
the same size and density as the original. Then follow these
steps:

1. Right-click on the Drive A object or the Drive B
object.

2. Click on Copy disk. An OS/2 window opens.

3. You'll see a message telling you to place the original diskette into the drive. Do so and press Enter.

4. At some point, you'll see a message telling you to remove the original diskette and to insert a target diskette for copying. Do that and press Enter.

Oops! Wrong Diskette!   If you see the message

SYS1340: Drive types or diskette types are incompatible.
Copy has ended.

it means you inserted a target diskette that was not the same density as the original. Get another diskette and start over.

5. When OS/2 is done copying the diskette, it will ask you if you want to **Copy Another Diskette (Y/N)?** If you do, press Y and Enter, and then insert the next original diskette. If you don't, press N and Enter. The window closes, and you're returned to OS/2 Warp.

In this lesson, you learned how to list the files on a diskette and how to format and copy a diskette. In the next lesson, you'll learn how to check the hard disk for problems and how to back up and restore files.

Lesson

14

Protecting Your Files

In this lesson, you'll learn how to check the hard disk for problems and how to back up and restore your files as needed.

Checking the Hard Disk for Problems

When your PC suddenly loses power or you reboot the PC yourself by pressing Ctrl+Alt+Delete, OS/2 does not have time to properly save your files. As a consequence, parts of discarded files (called *lost clusters* or *lost chains*) end up cluttering your hard disk. Therefore, from time to time, you should run CHKDSK to check for these problems. To do so, follow these steps:

1. Right-click on the Drive C object on the LaunchPad.

2. Click on the Check disk command. You'll see the Check Disk dialog box shown in Figure 14.1.

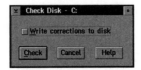

Figure 14.1 The Check Disk dialog box.

3. Click on the Check button. If CHKDSK finds a problem, it tells you so. When the process is complete, CHKDSK displays a results box.

4. Click on Cancel to close the box. Then click on Cancel in the Check Disk dialog box to close it too.

Although CHKDSK uncovers hard disk problems, it doesn't fix them. To have OS/2 fix any problems CHKDSK finds, follow these steps:

1. Click on the Shut down button on the LaunchPad.

2. When you see the message saying that it's safe to turn the PC off, insert the first emergency diskette and press Ctrl+Alt+Delete. (To create a set of emergency diskettes, see Lesson 13.)

3. Insert the second diskette when prompted. You won't be prompted, but insert the third emergency diskette anyway.

4. At the [**A:**] prompt, type CHKDSK C: /F and press Enter.

5. OS/2 will fix what it finds and then return you to the prompt. When you get back to the prompt, simply reboot to return to OS/2.

Backing Up Your Files

From time to time, you should back up your files to guard against data loss. If you have backups of your data and the original files get damaged somehow, you can restore the backups onto your computer—and you won't lose your work.

Back Up   A process that copies files onto a diskette in a special compressed format. Because the files are compressed, the diskette can hold more files with the BACKUP command than it can files written with the COPY command.

To backup all the files on your hard disk:

1. Insert the first emergency diskette into Drive A, and then reboot the PC by pressing Ctrl+Alt+Delete. (To create a set of emergency diskettes, see Lesson 13.)

2. Insert the second diskette when prompted. You won't be prompted, but insert the third emergency diskette anyway.

3. At the [A:\] prompt, type BACKUP C:*.* A: /S and press Enter.

4. You'll be prompted to place a diskette in Drive A. Do that and press Enter.

5. As the backup progresses, you'll be asked to replace that diskette with other diskettes until the entire hard disk is backed up.

Put your backup diskettes aside until you need them to restore some damaged files. If you want, you can reuse these diskettes the next time you do a complete system backup.

Performing a Periodic Backup

Once you've done a full system backup, you can do a periodic *maintenance backup* that backs up only files that have changed. This saves you the time of repeating a full system backup every week.

To perform a periodic backup, follow steps 1 and 2 in the steps for a regular backup. However, when you get to the [A:\] prompt, type BACKUP C:*.* A: /S /M /A and press Enter. Stick in your original backup diskettes when it asks for them, and Warp updates them to make them current.

Restoring Files After They've Been Damaged

Suppose the worst has happened. You try to open an important document, and you get the error message **Data error reading file**. Or worse still, all the files on your hard disk have somehow been damaged by the latest computer virus. Don't worry. Because you've created backups, you can restore good copies of those files from your backup diskettes.

> **Restore**   If the files on your hard disk get damaged somehow, you can restore them through a reverse backup process that decompresses the backed-up files and copies them back onto the hard disk.

To restore all the files on your hard disk, follow these steps. (If you want to restore only certain files and not the entire hard disk, see the next section.)

1. Insert the first emergency diskette into Drive A, and then reboot the PC by pressing Ctrl+Alt+Delete.

2. Insert the second diskette when prompted. You won't be prompted, but insert the third emergency diskette anyway.

3. At the [A:\] prompt, type **RESTORE A: C:*.* /S** and press Enter.

4. When prompted, place the first backup diskette in Drive A and press Enter.

5. As the restoration progresses, you'll be prompted to replace the first diskette with other diskettes until the entire drive is restored.

Restoring a Single Directory

If you're having problems with a particular directory, you
may want to restore only that directory and any subdirectories it might have. You don't have to boot with the emergency diskettes to restore a single directory unless the
directory you're trying to restore is the OS/2 directory.

To restore a single directory, such as the \PROJECTS
directory:

1. Open the OS/2 System folder. Then open the
   Command Prompts folder.

2. Double-click on the OS/2 Full Screen icon.

3. At the [C:\] prompt, type **RESTORE A:
   C:\PROJECTS*.*** /S and press Enter to restore the
   \PROJECTS directory and all of its subdirectories.

4. You'll be prompted to insert the backup diskette
   that contains the \PROJECTS directory. Do so and
   press Enter. Continue to insert diskettes as needed.

5. To return to OS/2 and close the window, type **EXIT**
   and press Enter.

In this lesson, you learned how to check your hard disk
for problems and fix those problems. You also learned how
to back up and restore your files. In the next lesson, you'll
learn how to start and stop a program.

Lesson 15

Starting and Exiting Programs

In this lesson, you'll learn how to start and stop a program and how to switch between programs.

Starting a Program

You can start a program in one of several ways:

- Double-click on its program object (its icon). If your new program doesn't have its own icon yet, refer to Lesson 25 for help creating one.

- Double-click on a data-file object associated with that program. (Generally, that means the data-file was created by the program you're trying to start.)

- Drag the appropriate *template* from the Templates folder into another folder or onto the Desktop. Then double-click on the resulting icon to start the program. For example, drag a Chart template out and double-click on it to start the charting program in IBM Works.

> **Templates** A template is like a form you fill in to create a new version of the template object. For example, you can use a template to create a new folder, a new letter, or a new spreadsheet.

If you don't like hunting through folders to find a program you want to start, you can add your favorite programs to the LaunchPad and then click just once to start them. See Lesson 16 for instructions on customizing the LaunchPad.

Starting Windows Programs You can start a Windows program without starting Windows itself by double-clicking on the program icon, or you can start Windows and launch Windows programs from there. To start Windows, double-click on either the WIN-OS/2 Full Screen icon or the WIN-OS/2 Window icon in the Command Prompts folder.

Starting DOS Programs If you want to start a DOS program, you don't have to jump to a DOS prompt. Just double-click on the appropriate icon. (In fact, don't start any program from a DOS prompt if you can help it; it really slows down your computer and can sometimes cause Warp to be really confused.)

Starting a Program Automatically

There's probably at least one program you use every single day. If so, you might want to set up OS/2 Warp to start that program every single time Warp starts. This saves you the time of looking for the file or icon and starting it yourself.

If you want to start a particular program each time you start OS/2 Warp, follow these steps:

1. Press and hold Ctrl+Shift.

2. Click on the program's icon with the right mouse button, and then drag its shadow over to the Startup folder (located inside the OS/2 System folder). A shadow, as you may recall, is a copy of an icon that points to the same file the original does.

Switching Between Programs

With OS/2, you can run lots of programs at the same time, and you can jump between them at will. Depending on the circumstances, there are multiple ways you can switch between windows.

- If you can see a portion of the window belonging to the program to which you want to jump, simply click on it. OS/2 brings that program to the top of your window pile.

- If you can't see the program window you want, click on the Window list button on the LaunchPad or press Ctrl+Esc to display the Window list. (You can also click both mouse buttons on the Desktop to display the Window list.) From the list, double-click on the program to which you want to switch. (See Figure 15.1.)

Double-click on the program to which you want to switch.

Figure 15.1   The Window list.

- If you're running WIN-OS/2 in a full-screen session, pressing Ctrl+Esc brings up the Task List. You can use it to switch between running Windows programs. To switch over to an OS/2 or DOS program while in a WIN-OS/2 full-screen session, press

Alt+Esc instead. (You can also click on the OS/2 icon at the bottom of your WIN-OS/2 screen to switch over to OS/2 without closing down Windows.)

Stopping a Program

When you're finished with a program, you should stop it (shut it down). Doing so reduces the amount of window clutter on your screen and makes your other programs run faster, because OS/2 has less to keep track of.

Follow these steps to shut down a program:

1. Save all your work first (see Lesson 17).

2. Exit the program by double-clicking on the title-bar icon, shown in Figure 15.2. If you're in a DOS program that's running in a window, double-click on the title-bar icon as usual. If you're in a full-screen DOS session, open the File menu and select Exit.

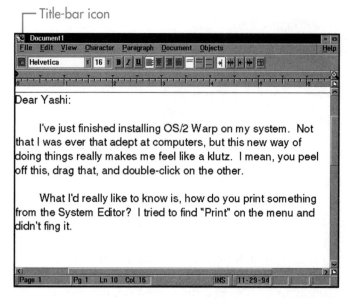

Figure 15.2 Exit a program by double-clicking on its title-bar icon.

There Is No Title-Bar Icon!   In a
Windows program, you double-click on the
Control-menu box (which is in the same
place the OS/2 title-bar icon usually is) to
exit a program.

Stopping Lots of Programs at Once   If
you're trying to close down a lot of programs at
once, just call up the Window list (by clicking on
the Window List button or pressing Ctrl+Esc). Select
the programs you want to stop by pressing Ctrl and
clicking on them. Then press Delete.

In this lesson, you learned how to start and stop programs. In the next lesson, you'll learn how to customize the
LaunchPad.

Lesson 16

Working with the LaunchPad

In this lesson, you'll learn how to use the LaunchPad and how to customize it by adding icons, deleting icons, changing the icon size, and so on.

How the LaunchPad Works

The LaunchPad, shown in Figure 16.1, keeps the objects you use the most close by, where they belong. You can use the buttons on the LaunchPad to switch between programs, lock up your PC while you step away from your desk for a moment, locate a missing icon, get help, print or delete your work, switch to DOS, or examine your files.

The left side of the LaunchPad contains action buttons, such as Lockup. The right side contains object buttons, which represent devices or programs. Each of the five object buttons has a drawer associated with it. You can place additional objects in these drawers to expand the capabilities of the LaunchPad. You can add more buttons (which can have one drawer apiece) to the LaunchPad itself. There's no real limit to the number of buttons you can add to the LaunchPad, but you might want to limit them in order to keep the LaunchPad a reasonable size.

Click on a drawer
handle to open a drawer.

Click on a button to
activate (open) that object.

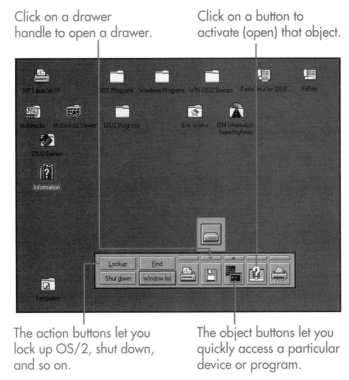

The action buttons let you
lock up OS/2, shut down,
and so on.

The object buttons let you
quickly access a particular
device or program.

Figure 16.1   The LaunchPad.

Two of these drawers already contain a button. For
example, in Figure 16.1, the Drive A drawer is open, revealing the Drive C button. In addition, the OS/2 Prompt Window drawer contains a button for the DOS Prompt Window.
You can add additional buttons to any of the drawers; for
example, you might want to add a Drive B button to the
Drive A drawer. Or you can add a button to the LaunchPad.
It's best to keep similar buttons together for convenience.

By the way, if you don't want to use some of the standard buttons on the LaunchPad, you can easily delete them,
as you'll learn in the next section. You can customize the
LaunchPad in other ways, too. For example, you can change

the size of the buttons, display the icons as text instead of icons and vice versa, or display the LaunchPad vertically.

The following list teaches you the basics of using the LaunchPad:

- To activate a button, simply click on it. For example, to shut down the PC, click on the Shut down button.

- If a button represents a device object (such as the Printer or the Shredder), drag another object over to that button and drop it. The action of that device is carried out on the object you dragged to it (for example, the object would be printed or deleted). Likewise, if you drag an object to the Drive A button, it is copied to a diskette in drive A.

- If you click on a device object button, a window appears to provide information about that object. For example, you could click on the Printer button to see what's currently in line to print.

- To open a drawer (and reveal the buttons inside), click on the drawer handle. A triangle appears on a drawer handle when its drawer contains buttons.

- To close the drawer, click on the handle again.

- To bring the LaunchPad into view, double-click inside an open window or on the Desktop.

- To move the LaunchPad, right-click in an open area between the buttons and drag it to its new location.

- You can disconnect a drawer from the LaunchPad by opening it and dragging it away. Use this feature to get the button(s) in the drawer closer to where you're working. When you want to reattach the drawer, just close and then reopen the LaunchPad drawer handle (by clicking on it twice), and the drawer reappears.

Adding and Deleting a Button

To add a button to the LaunchPad, follow these steps:

1. Right-click on the object you want to add to the LaunchPad.

2. Drag the object over to the LaunchPad. You'll see a dark line when you drag the object between two buttons (see Figure 16.2). This indicates that OS/2 understands what you want to do, which is—in this case—to add a shadow of the icon to the LaunchPad. (The original icon remains in its folder.)

> **Adding a Button to a Drawer** If you want to add your program button to a drawer (instead of placing it between two existing buttons), drag the icon over to a drawer handle and let go. When you want use your icon later, you'll have to click to open the drawer.

Drag your icon between two buttons and drop it.

Figure 16.2 Adding a button to the LaunchPad.

3. Release the mouse button, and your new button appears on the LaunchPad where you indicated.

To delete a button from the LaunchPad, follow these steps:

1. Right-click on the button.

2. Drag the button to the Shredder button.

3. Release the mouse button. Again, because the button is simply a shadow of the original icon, you're not really deleting the actual program icon.

Other Ways to Customize the LaunchPad

The LaunchPad has only one real drawback: it can easily get lost beneath other open windows. Although you can quickly display the LaunchPad by double-clicking inside any window or in an open area of the Desktop, you might prefer to keep it "on top of" all open windows all the time. If so, follow these steps:

1. Move the mouse pointer over a blank area of the LaunchPad (not over an object) and click the right mouse button.

2. Click on Settings.

3. Click on the Float on top option.

4. Double-click on the title-bar icon to close the Settings box.

Actually, the LaunchPad has one other drawback: by default, it leaves its drawers open all the time. For example, if you open a drawer and click on a button to use what's in it (as you might do with the Drive C object), you have to go back later and click on the drawer handle to close it. If you find this annoying, use the Settings command to change it, as described here:

1. Right-click on a blank area of the LaunchPad and click on Settings to open the Settings notebook.

2. Click on the Close drawer after object open option.

3. Double-click on the title-bar icon to close the Settings box. From now on, when you open a drawer to start a program (or whatever), LaunchPad automatically closes the drawer for you instead of leaving it open.

Regardless of whether or not you choose to float the LaunchPad on top of all windows, you can display the LaunchPad vertically (along the left or right side of the screen). To do so, follow these steps:

1. Right-click on a blank area of the LaunchPad and click on Settings to open the Settings notebook.

2. Click on the Display vertical option.

3. Double-click on the title-bar icon to close the Settings box. The LaunchPad appears vertically, as shown in Figure 16.3.

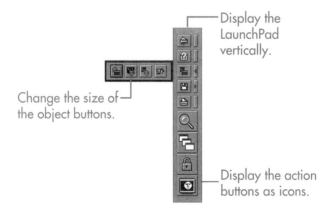

Figure 16.3 Customize the LaunchPad however you want.

You can change the size of the object buttons and the action buttons if you want. You can also display the action buttons as icons instead of text (such as Shut down and Lockup), and you can display the object buttons as text instead of icons (such as the picture of the Printer). These steps show you how to make any of these types of changes:

1. Right-click on a blank area of the LaunchPad and click on Settings to open the Settings notebook.

2. To change the size of the object buttons, click on the Small icons option. To display the object buttons as text, click on the Display text in drawers option and/or the Display text on LaunchPad option.

3. To change the size of the action buttons, click on the arrow at the bottom of the page to move to page two. Then click on either the Display action buttons as mini-icons option or the Display action buttons as normal icons option. You can choose to not display the action buttons at all by clicking on the Do not display action buttons option.

4. Double-click on the title-bar icon to close the Settings box. The LaunchPad reflects whatever changes you put into effect. Figure 16.3 contains examples of some of these options.

In this lesson, you learned how to use and customize the LaunchPad. In the next lesson, you'll learn how to open, save, and print files.

Lesson

Working with Your Programs

In this lesson, you'll learn how to open, save, and print a file from within your programs. You'll also learn how to create a new file with a template.

Opening a File to Edit

Once you have started your program (see Lesson 15), you're ready to create something new, but if you want to change a file you've already saved, you have to open it first. When you open a file, you tell the program which file you want to edit, and the program places its contents on-screen so you can make changes to it.

To open a file, follow these steps:

1. Open the File menu and select Open. The File Open dialog box, shown in Figure 17.1, appears.

2. If necessary, change to the drive that contains the file you want to edit by selecting one from the Drive drop-down list.

3. Change to the directory that contains the file by scrolling through the Directory list and double-clicking on the directory you want. When you choose a directory, its files appear in the Files list on the left.

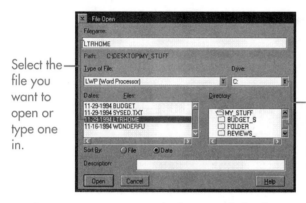

Select the file you want to open or type one in.

Select the drive and directory that contains the file you want to open.

Figure 17.1   A typical File Open dialog box.

4. Under Filename, type the name of the file you want to open or select one from the Files list.

5. Click on Open. The program opens your file and displays it on-screen, ready to edit.

Using a Template to Create a New File

With a template, you can create data-file objects of a particular type. Just "tear" the appropriate template from its pad and fill in the necessary information to create a letter, a sales spreadsheet, or a client database. Here's how:

1. Double-click on the Templates folder.

2. Right-click on the template you want. For example, right-click on the Data File template icon.

3. Drag the template-form onto the Desktop or into a folder, as shown in Figure 17.2. A data-file object appears with a generic name such as "Chart," "Document," or "Data File."

4. To give your new file a name, press Alt and click on the data-file object. Drag over the generic name, and then type a name for your new file. Click anywhere on the Desktop to save the name.

Drag a template into a folder and rename it.

Then double-click on it to start the program and create your file.

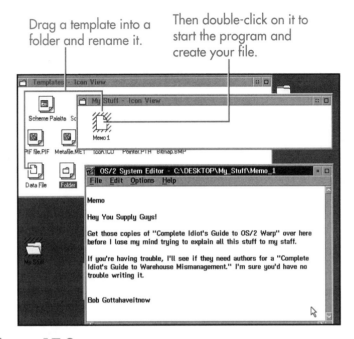

Figure 17.2 Use a template to create a new file.

5. Double-click on the new data-file object to start the appropriate program. For example, double-click on the Data File object to start the OS/2 System Editor.

6. Enter your data into the file.

Creating Your Own Templates

You can create your own templates, too, and reuse them just like the templates that come with OS/2. The following steps show you how to create your own template:

1. Create your letter, memo, or whatever as usual.

2. Type only the text you want to reuse every time you create something like it. (For example, in a letter template, you might want to include only your name, address, and a generic greeting.)

3. Save your "template" data-file and exit the program.

4. Click on the data-file object with the right mouse button and select Settings from the menu.

5. Click on the General tab and select Template. Double-click on the title-bar icon to close the Settings notebook. The icon for your data-file changes to look like a template icon.

6. Drag the new template over to the Templates folder so you can keep all your templates together.

From now on, you can use your template over and over.

Saving Your Changes

After you make changes to a file, you should save them. If you don't save your changes and either you exit the program or the power to your PC accidentally goes out, you'll lose all your work. So save as you go, and then save again before you exit.

To save a file, follow these steps:

1. Open the File menu and select Save. If you've never saved this file before, the dialog box shown in Figure 17.3 appears. (If you're working in a DOS or Windows program, your Save As box will look a bit different. Follow these same steps to save your file.)

2. Type a file name. Type a period and add an extension if you need to (most programs provide the extension for you).

> **What Can I Name It?**   What you can name a file depends on the type of file system (FAT or HPFS) you use. See Lesson 11 for more details.

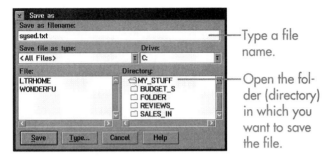

—Type a file name.

—Open the folder (directory) in which you want to save the file.

Figure 17.3 Save your work often.

3. Change the Drive and Directory if you want to save this file in a particular folder (directory).

4. Click on Save.

I've Saved the File, Now What?   Just keep right on working and save again whenever you feel you need to. Or you can exit the program by double-clicking on the title-bar icon.

Printing Your Work

Once you've saved your file, you can print it if you want. Depending on your situation, you have multiple options for printing a file. For example, if you've already left the program and saved your file, here's how to print it:

- Drag the data-file object to the Printer object to print it.

- To fax a document instead of printing it, drag the data-file object over to the FxPrint object (provided you installed the FaxWorks program from the BonusPak; see the inside back cover for more help on that one).

But what if you're still *in* the program?

• If you're using an OS/2 program, you'll need to save the file and exit the program. Then you can drag the data-file object to the Printer object. Sorry if you're used to a File Print command like Windows and DOS programs use; OS/2 just doesn't do it that way.

• If you're using IBM Works, you *can* print the file while you're still in the program. Just drag the Print icon over to the printer.

• If you're using a DOS or a Windows program, you can print from within the program by opening the File menu and selecting the Print command. If you've already saved the file and exited the program, you can use the drag-and-drop method described earlier.

In this lesson, you learned how to open, save, and print a file. You also learned how to work with templates. In the next lesson, you'll learn how to share data between programs.

Lesson

Copying and Moving Data Between Programs

In this lesson, you'll learn how to copy or move data between OS/2, Windows, and DOS programs.

With Warp, you can share, copy, or move data between DOS, Windows, and OS/2 programs. When you copy data, the original data remains intact and the copy is placed where you indicate (in a different file or in a different location within the same file). When you move data, the original data is deleted from its original location and placed at the new location.

In addition to copying and moving data, you can *link* (share) data. When you link data, any changes you later make to the original data are made automatically to the linked document. OS/2 performs this bit of magic with something it calls the *Clipboard*, a waiting area in memory where it holds data that is being copied or moved someplace else.

Be Prepared to Lose Formatting When you use the Clipboard to copy or move data between documents in different programs, you lose any special formatting along the way (such as bold or italics). For example, if you try to copy the words *BIG BOLD TEXT* from one document into another, all you'll get is BIG BOLD TEXT.

How Do I Know What's Currently on the Clipboard? You can view the contents of the Clipboard with the Clipboard Viewer, located in the Productivity folder (which is tucked away in the OS/2 System folder).

Setting Up OS/2 to Share

To copy or move data between OS/2 and DOS programs, you use the OS/2 Clipboard. Windows also has a Clipboard, which is used to share data between Windows programs.

The Windows Clipboard (more properly called the WIN-OS/2 Clipboard) can be set up to share its data with the OS/2 Clipboard, that is, whatever data is placed on one Clipboard is automatically copied to the other. This "link" between the two clipboards makes it possible for you to copy data between OS/2, Windows, and even DOS programs whenever you want.

Ordinarily, the link between the two clipboards is turned off. To share data between OS/2 and Windows, turn on the link as described here:

1. Open the OS/2 System folder and open the System Setup folder.

2. Right-click on the WIN-OS/2 Setup icon and select Settings.

3. Click on the Data Exchange tab.

4. Verify that the Clipboard and DDE options are set to Public.

5. Click on the Session tab.

6. Click on the WIN-OS/2 settings option and click on OK.

7. Verify that the WIN-DDE and the WIN-CLIPBOARD options are set to ON and click on Save.

8. Close the Settings notebook by double-clicking on the title-bar icon.

Working with a Windows or OS/2 Program

To copy or move data from a Windows or OS/2 program, you must select the data first. Use one of these two methods to do that:

- To select *text*, click in front of the first word you want. Hold down the left mouse button and drag the mouse over the rest of the text you want to select. The text turns darker to show that you've selected it.

- To select a *graphic*, click in the middle of it. The graphic will be surrounded by tiny boxes called *handles* that let you know you've selected it.

   Once you've selected your data, here's how to copy or move it:

1. Select what you want to copy or move.

2. Press Ctrl+Insert to *copy* or Shift+Delete to *cut* (move) the data. You can use the Edit Copy or Edit Cut command if you want to use the menus.

3. Switch to the other program and click where you want the data to appear.

4. Finally, press Shift+Insert or use the Edit Paste command to copy what's on the Clipboard into your document.

One at a Time! You can store only *one thing* (text or graphics) on the Clipboard at a time. So if you want to copy or move data, make sure you complete the task (paste it into the new location) before you do anything else. When you cut or copy something else to the Clipboard, it replaces whatever is already there.

Note, however, that because the data on the Clipboard stays there until it's replaced, you can paste the same thing over and over in several different documents or in several places of one document.

Working with a DOS Program

You can only copy data from a DOS program; you cannot move it. To move data, you must copy it first, and then return to the original document and delete the data. To copy data from a DOS program, follow these steps:

It Must Be in a Window For your DOS program to use the Clipboard, the DOS program must be running in a window, and not in a full-screen session.

1. If necessary, put your full-screen DOS program in a window by pressing Alt+Home.

2. Now click on the title-bar icon and select Mark from the window menu.

3. Click in front of the first word you want to copy. Hold down the left mouse button and drag the pointer over the rest of the text you want to select, as shown in Figure 18.1.

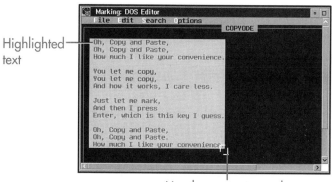

Highlighted text

Use the cursor to mark (select) your text.

Figure 18.1 Copying data from a DOS program may look a bit strange, but it works.

4. Press Enter. This copies your selection to the Clipboard.

5. Switch to the other program and click where you want the data to appear.

6. Finally, press Shift+Insert to copy what's on the Clipboard into your document.

If you're copying data into another DOS program, make sure it is in a window. Then click on the title-bar icon and select Paste from the menu which appears. (Shift+Insert will not work in the DOS program.)

Isn't This Like Windows?   Yes. If you were using Windows instead of OS/2 Warp, you'd follow these same steps to copy data from a DOS program. So if you're used to Windows, there's a good chance you're already familiar with this procedure.

Linking Data

Linking data is similar to copying it, but when you link data, the data is updated automatically in the second document when you change it in the original.

> **It Won't Work!**   If you're having trouble getting this to work, right-click on the WIN-OS/2 Setup object and select Data Exchange. In the Settings notebook, make sure that the DDE option is set to Public. Then check your documentation to be sure that both of the programs you're trying to link support *DDE*, which is the fancy name for this linking business.

To link data from one document to another:

1. Select the data you want to link, and then copy it to the Clipboard by pressing Ctrl+Insert.

2. Switch to the other document, but *don't* press Shift+Insert.

3. Open the Edit menu and select the Link, Paste Special command or the Paste Link command. (They're called different things in different programs.)

4. If you get a dialog box, click on the Link button or the Paste Link button, and you're done.

Now if you return to the original document and change something, it's changed automatically in the second document.

Using OLE to Embed Data

OLE (pronounce *oh-LAY*) stands for *object linking and embedding*, and it's something Windows programs do. Warp programs have their own version of OLE called SOM (pro-nounced "some," it's short for *system object model*).

With OLE or SOM, you *embed* your data instead of linking it. Embedding creates an invisible link to the original program. Then, if you're working in the second document and you need to make changes to the data, you just double-click on it. The original program starts up so you can edit the embedded data. When you're done, you quit that program, and you're returned to your document.

No Mixing and Matching   Will this work between Windows and OS/2? No. OLE works only between two Windows programs that support it, and SOM works only between two OS/2 programs.

Follow these steps to embed data with OLE or SOM:

1. Select the data you want to embed.

2. Open the Edit menu and select Copy.

3. Switch to the second program, open the Edit menu, and select Paste Special.

4. Click on Paste to embed your object.

Now, when you feel like changing the object from within the second document, just double-click on it. What happens next depends on the application: either you'll find yourself in the original application, or you'll remain in your second application but the tools from the original application will appear so you can make changes. Once you've made your changes, exit the program, and you are returned to the document.

In this lesson you learned how to copy, move, link, and embed data. In the next lesson, you'll learn how to run Windows and DOS programs under OS/2.

Lesson

19

Running Windows and DOS Under OS/2

In this lesson, you'll learn how to run Windows and DOS programs in OS/2 Warp.

With OS/2 Warp, you can run your Windows programs in any of three ways:

- By starting Windows itself and then launching your programs from there.

- By starting Windows in a window on the OS/2 Desktop and launching your programs from there. Running Windows in a window makes it easy to use both Windows and OS/2 programs at the same time without a lot of running around.

- By launching your Windows programs from the OS/2 Desktop, without actually starting Windows.

You can also run your DOS programs in any of three ways:

- By starting your DOS program in a window. Again, using a window makes it easier to interact with all your OS/2, Windows, and DOS programs.

- By starting your DOS program in a full-screen session. This makes your DOS program easier to see because it takes up the entire screen.

- By starting your DOS program from a command line prompt. (Although this is not the best way to start

DOS programs, you'll learn that there are other reasons why you might want to use a command prompt.)

This lesson shows you in detail how to use all these methods to run your Windows and DOS programs.

Running Windows Itself

To start Windows in a full-screen session:

1. Open the OS/2 System folder, and then open the Command Prompts folder.

2. Double-click on the WIN-OS/2 Full Screen icon.

3. If you want to start a Windows program, just double-click on it.

> **Switching Between Programs** To switch between Windows programs, press Ctrl+Esc to display Windows' Task List, and then double-click on a program. To switch to an OS/2 program, press Alt+Esc to display OS/2's Desktop, click on the Window list button on the LaunchPad, and then double-click on a program to switch to it.

When you run Windows "full-screen," the Windows Desktop takes up the entire screen just as it would if you were running Windows only. The only difference is that the small OS/2 Desktop icon appears at the bottom. Here are some tips on using this version of Windows with OS/2:

• Double-click on the OS/2 Desktop icon to switch to the OS/2 Desktop. (See Figure 19.1.) When you do this, Windows isn't shut down; it and all your Windows programs remain running.

• To switch back to the full-screen Windows session from OS/2, click on the Window list button on the

LaunchPad. Then double-click on WIN-OS/2 Full Screen.

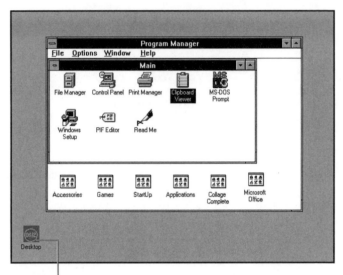

Double-click here to switch to OS/2.

Figure 19.1   Switching back to OS/2 is easy.

* To exit Windows completely, shut down all your Windows programs. Then click on the Program Manager's File menu and select Exit Windows.

Running Windows in a Window

Running Windows within a window makes it easier to switch between your OS/2 and Windows programs:

1. Open the OS/2 System folder, and then open the Command Prompts folder.

2. Double-click on the WIN-OS/2 Window icon. Windows starts up in a window right on the OS/2 Desktop, as shown in Figure 19.2.

Another Way?   You can also start Windows in a window by double-clicking on the Program Manager icon in the Windows Programs folder.

The OS/2 Desktop

Program Manager running in an OS/2 window

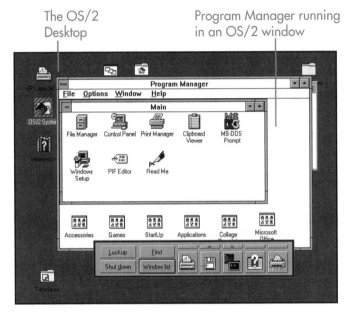

Figure 19.2   Running Windows in a window.

Program Manager behaves here just as it would on the Windows Desktop, with two small exceptions. First, if you click on the Minimize button, don't expect Program Manager to turn up as an icon at the bottom of your screen. Instead, it acts just like any other OS/2 window when you minimize it and goes into hiding. Access the Window list (press Alt+Esc) and double-click on WIN-OS/2 window: session to switch back to Windows after you minimize it. Second, when you exit Program Manager, you don't end up at a DOS prompt the way you would if you were running real Windows. Instead, you merely shut down the Windows session and return to the OS/2 Desktop.

To close down the window (and shut down Windows), simply double-click on the Control-menu box, or open the File menu and select Exit Windows.

> **What a Drag**   Remember that while you're working within the boundaries of the Windows window, you must use the left mouse button to drag. If you start working on the OS/2 Desktop, use the *right* mouse button to drag.

Running Windows Programs Without Running Windows

You can run your Windows programs without starting Windows first. To do so, follow these steps:

1. Open the folder that contains the Windows program you want to run. You'll find the Windows freebies (such as the Control Panel, Print Manager, and Clipboard Viewer) in the Windows Programs folder. Your own Windows programs are in the WIN-OS/2 Groups folder.

2. Double-click on the program icon. The Windows program starts in a window on the OS/2 Desktop.

> **Where's My Program's Icon?**   If you've just installed a new Windows program, you need to create its icon before you can use it. See Lesson 25 for help.

Running DOS Programs

Although there are multiple methods you can use to run DOS programs, it's actually quite simple. Here's how:

- To start the program, simply double-click on the program icon. The program starts in a full-screen session, which makes it easier for you to view.

- To change a DOS program so that it always starts in a windowed session (instead of full-screen), right-click on the program icon and select Settings. Click on the Session tab and select DOS window.

- To switch from a windowed session to a full-screen session (or vice versa), press Alt+Home. (If you click on the Maximize button, the window only fills three-quarters of the screen.)

- You can also switch from a windowed session to a full-screen session by clicking on the title-bar icon and selecting Full-Screen from the Window menu.

When you finish using a DOS program, you can stop the program just as easily as you started it. To exit the program, open the program's File menu and select Exit or double-click on the title-bar icon.

> **What If the Program Garfs?**   You might need to change some of the settings for the DOS program (see Lesson 25). If that doesn't work, you can always boot to DOS and then start the program. If you have to do that, see the next section for help.

Booting to DOS

Sometimes you may want to start DOS instead of OS/2. For example, you might choose to do this to run a DOS program that doesn't run well under OS/2, or when you want to run a DOS utility, such as an anti-virus or hard disk utility. In that case, simply boot to DOS and then start your program, as described here:

1. From OS/2 Warp, close down all programs.

2. Open the OS/2 System folder and open the Command Prompts folder.

3. Double-click on the Dual Boot icon.

4. A window appears, asking you if you wish to continue. Press Y for Yes and press Enter. The system restarts at a DOS prompt, C:\>.

5. Run your DOS program. To return to OS/2, exit your program, type C:\OS2\BOOT /OS2 at the C:\> prompt, and press Enter.

6. The system restarts and displays the OS/2 Desktop. You'll see a window similar to the one in step 4, asking you if you want to boot to DOS. Press N for No and press Enter to close Dual Boot.

> **No Dual Boot Icon?** If you don't have a Dual Boot icon, you must have installed Boot Manager. In that case, simply shut down as normal, restart the system, and select DOS from the menu. You can also boot to DOS by following the steps to display the [A:\] prompt given in the section "Checking Your Hard Disk for Problems" in Lesson 14.

Getting to a Command Line Prompt

A command prompt is simply a series of characters that *prompt* you to enter a command. They usually look like C:\> or [C:\]. To use a command prompt, you just type the command you want and press Enter.

Warp provides two command lines: the DOS prompt, C:\>, and an OS/2 prompt, [C:\]. You're better off using the OS/2 command prompt, since it allows you to use both DOS and OS/2 commands. But remember, only go to a command prompt when you have to. Most of the time, you can accomplish anything you want to do from the OS/2 Desktop.

Why Use the Prompt?   Use the prompt to enter certain DOS commands such as UNDELETE, BACKUP (to backup the entire hard disk, boot to DOS first), CHKDSK, and MEM. You can also install DOS programs or start them from the prompt.

Follow these steps to display the OS/2 prompt:

1. Click on the OS/2 Prompt button on the LaunchPad. A window appears, as shown in Figure 19.3.

2. Type the command at the prompt and press Enter.

3. To close the window and return to OS/2, type Exit after the prompt and press Enter.

Things You Shouldn't Do While Using a Command Prompt

There are some commands you *shouldn't* enter at an OS/2 or DOS prompt because they might get OS/2 very confused.

DEFRAG or some other disk optimizer   Because these rearrange files on the hard disk, they'll confuse any programs you have running, including OS/2 itself.

If your drive is a FAT drive and not HPFS, you can use these if you reboot your system to DOS.

Programs that do funny things to the hard disk   Don't run any of your old DOS utilities (such as anti-virus or disk-fixers) unless you're sure your drive is a FAT drive. Also, you won't be able to run these things unless you boot to DOS.

Any command that starts a program   Some DOS programs freak out if you start them at the prompt and not with a start button (icon).

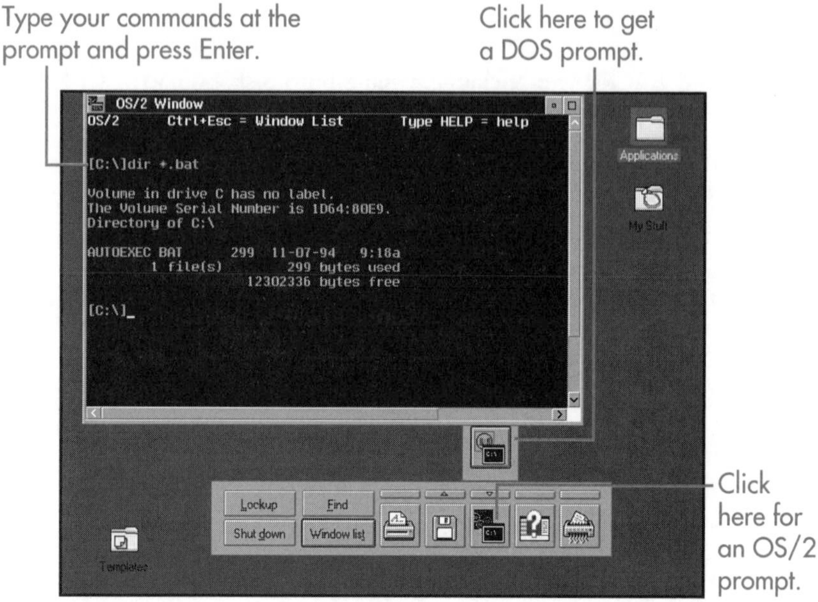

Type your commands at the prompt and press Enter.

Click here to get a DOS prompt.

Click here for an OS/2 prompt.

Figure 19.3 OS/2 provides two command prompts.

DoubleSpace, DriveSpace, or some other disk compression program Even if you boot to DOS, don't use these because they may corrupt your files.

In this lesson, you learned how to run Windows and DOS programs. In the next lesson, you'll learn how to connect to the Internet with OS/2 Warp.

Lesson 20

Connecting to the Internet

In this lesson, you'll learn how to use OS/2 Warp to connect to the Internet.

What Is the Internet?

The Internet is a group of connected *networks*. In fact, it's the largest collection of interconnected networks in the world, including government agencies, universities, military installations, scientific research centers, and large businesses (including Macmillan Computer Publishing) located all over the world. The various networks that make up the Internet have only agreed to make their information available; if you don't know how to get it or use it, tough. They're not obligated to provide you with any help, so they usually don't— which means the Internet is no place for the timid.

> **Network** A group of computers connected to each other for the purpose of sharing data, programs, and printers.

Still, learning to use the Internet is worth the trouble. Once you've connected to the Internet, you can search for whatever information interests you, ranging from the scientific (such as the migratory patterns of birds) to the more common (such as the latest on the O.J. Simpson trial). You can download (receive) files, carry on a typed "conversation" about a topic of interest, send some e-mail, or just browse.

Getting Connected

To connect to the Internet, you must set up an account with a *service provider* (a company directly connected to the Internet that allows you to connect to the Net through them—for a fee, of course). With OS/2, you can connect to the Internet in one of several ways:

- Through the IBM Internet Connection. You still pay a fee for the service, but since OS/2 Warp is precon-figured to connect you to this, it's probably the simplest option.

- Through a local service provider with a *dial-in direct* (SLIP) account. You can easily set up access with your own service provider within OS/2. However, you cannot currently connect through a network account; so if your office is connected directly to the Internet, you won't be able to use Warp to connect through it.

- Through an online service, such as America Online or Delphi. If you do this, you'll most likely use the programs that the service provides to you, not the ones that come with OS/2 Warp (which I explain how to use in Lesson 21).

Setting Up the Connection to IBM

Follow these steps to connect to the Internet using the IBM Connection *for the first time*:

1. Open the IBM Information Superhighway folder. Open the IBM Internet Connection for OS/2 folder.

2. Double-click on the IBM Internet Dialer.

3. Click on Register. Then click on Open a personal account, read the contract, and click on OK.

4. Enter your basic information: name, address, and credit card number. Click on OK.

5. Continue entering additional information such as your modem type, COM port, and so on.

6. Enter three choices for a user ID, which the program will check against the master list once you're connected. Click OK.

7. Finally, click on Send registration to IBM.

8. The modem dials, connects, and flashes another agreement, and then lists the charges. Click on Yes I agree to conditions. The Dialer gives you your user ID, password, and e-mail address. *Write these down!* Then click OK.

9. OS/2 tries to find a local number for you to dial. Select a backup access number if there is one in your area in case the first service goes out at noon the day you have to finish that research project for your boss. Then click OK.

You're returned to the Internet Registration screen, and you're registered to use the IBM Internet Connection.

Connecting to IBM

To connect to the Internet after you're registered, simply double-click on the IBM Internet Dialer. When prompted, enter your password and click OK. Once you're connected, the service might attempt to download the latest additions to OS/2 Warp. When it's finished, minimize the window, and you're ready to use the OS/2 utilities. (See Lesson 21.)

When you want to disconnect from the Internet, restore the window and click on the Hang up button.

Setting Up the Connection to Another Service Provider

If you choose to get a local Internet provider, shop around for the best services and the best price. (You can find lots of providers listed in *The Complete Idiot's Guide to the Internet*, or you can check your local Yellow Pages under Internet, Computer Services, or Network Services.)

From your service provider, get a user ID, password, and phone number for the service. You might want them to remain on the phone as you complete the connection information, as outlined here:

1. Open the IBM Information Superhighway folder. Open the IBM Internet Connection for OS/2 folder. Open the Internet Utilities folder.

2. Double-click the Dial Other Internet Providers icon.

3. Have your service provider help you complete the four pages of information. Click on Next to go from page to page, and then click on OK when you're set up.

Connecting to Your Service Provider

To connect to your service provider, follow these steps:

1. Open the IBM Information Superhighway folder. Open the IBM Internet Connection for OS/2 folder. Open the Internet Utilities folder.

2. Double-click the Dial Other Internet Providers icon.

3. Select your provider from the list and click on Dial.

4. Once connected, minimize the window, and you're ready to use the OS/2 utilities. (See Lesson 21.) When you want to disconnect, restore the window and click on the Hang up button.

In this lesson, you learned how to connect to the Internet with OS/2 Warp. In the next lesson, you'll learn how to use the Internet utilities included with OS/2.

Navigating the Internet Cyberhighway

In this lesson, you'll learn how to use the Internet utilities included with OS/2 Warp.

IBM provides lots of tools that help you get the most out of the Internet. Let's take a quick tour and explore them all. (I can't hope to cover everything about the Internet in this book, so I recommend that you grab a copy of *The Complete Idiot's Guide to the Internet*—and when you want to know more, *The Complete Idiot's Next Step with the Internet*—by Peter Kent.)

> **Make Sure You Log Off!** Closing down any of the Internet tools does *not* log you off of the Internet. To do that, you must click on the Hang up button from within the IBM Internet Dialer window or the Dial Other Internet Provider window.

Sending E-Mail

To send someone e-mail (electronic mail), you need the electronic address that they use through the Internet or some online service. An Internet address consists of a *login name* and a *domain name*. For example, my address is **jfulton@alpha.mcp.com**.

To send e-mail, follow these steps:

1. Open the Ultimedia Mail/2 Lite folder in the IBM Internet Connection for OS/2 folder.

2. Double-click on the New Letter icon.

3. Under To:, type the address of the person you want to e-mail (see Figure 21.1). Later on, you can use the Names and Addresses icon in the Ultimedia Mail/2 Lite folder to save your favorite addresses; then you can pop them in here by clicking on the Names button.

Figure 21.1   Sending e-mail.

4. Type a subject, such as "Loved your book!"

5. Click in the text area. Select the "signature" at the top of the letter area and replace it with your own, such as "Jennifer Fulton, Alpha Books." If you want, you can set up your permanent signature by selecting Letter Settings and typing the signature again.

6. Press Enter a few times and then type your message. When necessary, press Enter to advance to the next line, just as you would on a typewriter.

7. Click on the Send button. A copy of the letter is saved in the Sent Mail folder, located in the Mail Cabinet folder.

> **Save Money!**   Start Ultimedia Lite/2 Lite *without* connecting to the Internet, compose your mail, and then click on Send. You'll be prompted to connect at that time.

To check on your own mail, double-click on the In-basket icon (it's in the Ultimedia Mail/2 Lite folder). If you're still in the Letter window, just open the Windows menu and select In-basket instead. To exit the program, double-click on the title-bar icon.

Locating Things That Interest You with Gopher

Gopher is a program that helps you connect to various Internet sites through a simple-to-use menu system. To use Gopher, follow these steps:

1. Double-click on the Gopher icon. You should see the Gopher menu for your host site (your service provider).

2. Double-click on a gopher to see a submenu of further items. A magnifying glass icon lets you search for files. If you find a document icon (it looks like a piece of paper), double-click on it to view it.

3. To go back to the previous menu, press Esc.

4. If you find something you like, download it. Just click on it to select it, and then open the Selected menu and choose Get.

Click on a gopher...

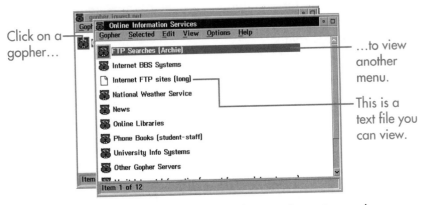

...to view another menu.

This is a text file you can view.

Figure 21.2 Gopher helps you locate information on the Internet.

5. To exit, open the Gopher menu and select Exit program. Then click on Yes.

While you're connected, you can switch to another Gopher server, some of which are listed on the Gopher menu under Well-Known Gopher Servers. If you know the address of a Gopher site, you can switch to it by opening the Gopher menu and selecting the command Specify Gopher Host.

How Do I Find Stuff? To search Gopher sites for a file, use Veronica (that is, if the site has an option for it).

Downloading Files with FTP-PM

An FTP site is a place on the Internet that contains a vast collection of files available to the general public. If you find a site that has a file you can use, you start up FTP-PM to *download* it (copy it to your hard disk). These steps walk you through the process in detail.

1. Open the Internet Utilities folder.

2. Double-click on the FTP-PM icon.

3. Under Host:, type the name of the site you want to search.

4. Under User:, try **anonymous**. For the Password:, type your own Internet address, such as jfulton@alpha.mcp.com.

5. Click on OK, and OS/2 tries to connect you to the FTP site. The top of the box shows your hard disk (the local host) and the bottom shows the FTP site (the remote host).

6. If you find a file you like, mark it by clicking on it. Repeat until you're done selecting files.

7. Change to the directory (folder) on your system (the local host) where you want your new files to go.

8. Click on QuickTrans on the menu. You can change the file names if you want to; otherwise, just click on Yes to start the downloading process.

Catching Up on News with NewsReader/2

Something else you can do on the Internet is browse *newsgroups*. Think of Internet newsgroups as large coffee rooms where you can catch up on things that interest you and share your opinions with other people. To access an Internet newsgroup, follow these steps:

1. Double-click on the NewsReader/2 icon in the IBM Connection for OS/2 folder.

2. You'll be asked whether you want a list of available newsgroups. Click on Yes.

3. Subscribe to the topics you like by double-clicking on them.

> **What Does It Cost?** Subscribing doesn't cost anything. By subscribing to a particular news-group, you make its information available to you during the session. Don't subscribe to a topic unless you're sure you want to bother with it. If you skipped something you're now interested in, open the File menu and select List all newsgroups. Then add more newsgroups to your permanent list.

4. Double-click on a newsgroup to view a list of articles/messages for that group.

5. From this list, double-click to view an article. You can view the next article by pressing N. Articles you've viewed are highlighted in the Article list.

6. If you want to reply to an article after viewing it, open the Actions menu and select Post reply. The original article appears with a > in front of it. Delete the parts of the original article that you don't need, and then type your response. Click on Post.

Connecting to a Telnet Site

Telnet switches you from your current site (the service provider) to another Internet site. However, the system you're switching to has to be friendly enough to let you in. If you do manage to connect to a Telnet site, try logging in as "anonymous" or "guest."

One reason for connecting to a Telnet site is to use Archie. Archie is an index system that helps you find files. Here's how to connect to a Telnet site and use Archie:

1. Open the Internet Utilities folder and double-click on the Telnet icon.

2. Open the Connection menu and select Open session.

3. Under Host name, type the name of an Archie site. For example, try one of these: **archie.ans.net** or **archie.internic.net**. You can type in the Port number (if you know it) and click OK.

4. To log in, type archie and press Enter. As long as the Telnet site has Archie, you'll see an **archie>** prompt.

5. Type prog os2. If there are any OS/2 files out there, you'll see a list (actually, quite a list). Press Spacebar to view more files or q to quit the listing and try another prog command. If you find something interesting, write down its location, and you can try downloading it with FTP.

6. When you're done Telnetting, type bye (or "quit" or "logout") to leave the Archie site. Then open the Connection menu and select Exit.

Wandering the World Wide Web

The WebExplorer allows you to navigate the Internet using the *World Wide Web.* Before I show you how to use WebExplorer, take a moment to make sure you've installed the Multimedia Viewer from the BonusPak—you're going to need it.

World Wide Web A series of graphical documents connected to each other on the Internet through a series of links called *hypertext.* You navigate from one web document to another through these hypertext links. Because of its graphical nature, the WWW makes finding information on the Internet easier.

Plain English

No WebExplorer? If your version of Warp did not come with the WebExplorer, you can easily download it. Just double-click on the Retrieve Software Updates icon in the IBM Internet Connection for OS/2 folder, and you're connected to IBM. Select WebExplorer from the list of files to download and select Install. WebExplorer installs itself. Once it's done, restart your system, and you're ready to go.

Follow these steps to connect to a Web site using WebExplorer:

1. Double-click on the WebExplorer icon. The first time you use WebExplorer, you'll see a message telling you that the EXPLORE.INI file is missing. Just click OK to bypass this message.

2. Click on the Load Home Page icon shown in Figure 21.3.

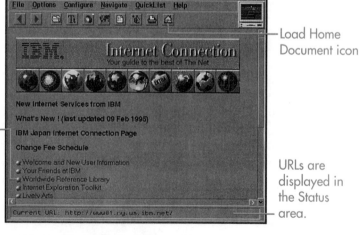

Load Home Document icon

Hypertext links are shown in blue.

URLs are displayed in the Status area.

Figure 21.3 The Web Explorer.

3. Navigate through the Internet by following any of the steps listed here.

4. Double-click on the title-bar icon to close the WebExplorer.

Once you've connected to a Web page, such as the IBM Internet Connection home page shown in Figure 21.3, you can jump to another Web page via a *hypertext link*. Hypertext links are displayed in blue. Click on one, and you're taken to the Web page it's linked to. Once you've viewed a link on a page, the hypertext is displayed in purple so you can keep track of where you've gone.

If you encounter any problems connecting to a page, press Esc or click on the Halt button to stop the page from loading.

> **What's a URL?**   URL stands for *universal resource locator*, and it's the address for a page on the Web. When you move the mouse pointer over a hypertext link, you'll see the URL (the address for the page it's linked to) in the Status area, as shown in Figure 21.3.

You can also use these icons when working (or playing) on the Web:

Icon	Function
◀	Moves backward in the WebMap.
▶	Moves forward in the WebMap.
▤	Opens a text window so you can specify a URL.
Tt	Enables you to select fonts.

continues

Continued

Icon	Function
	Enables you to select text and background color.
	Displays WebMap.
	Displays QuickList.
	Adds current document to QuickList.
	Prints current document.
	Loads home document.
	Stops page from loading.

In this lesson, you learned how to use the Internet utilities included with OS/2 Warp. In the next lesson, you'll learn how to handle word processing chores with the programs that come with OS/2.

Lesson

Word Processing

In this lesson, you'll learn how to use OS/2 Warp to handle your basic word processing chores.

The Three Editors That Come with OS/2 Warp

OS/2 provides many options when it comes to editing text. If you want to edit a configuration file, use the OS/2 System Editor. It's simple and straightforward and lets you do little more than move characters around (which, when dealing with a file like CONFIG.SYS, is all you want). If you want to write a memo or a report that includes formatting as bold, underline, or italics, use IBM Works or the Enhanced Editor.

Here's how to tell which of OS/2's editors you should use:

OS/2 System Editor   Use this to edit your configuration files (such as CONFIG.SYS and AUTOEXEC.BAT) or to read information files (such as README.TXT).

Enhanced Editor   Although you can write a letter or a memo with this editor, it's very difficult to do. Don't use it.

IBM Works   The perfect choice for creating letters, memos, reports, or whatever. It's easy to use.

How Does This Compare to Windows?   Windows comes with two editors, Write (which is similar to IBM Works) and Notepad (which is similar to the OS/2 System Editor). Choose the option that is most like what you used to use.

Entering Text

To enter text into a file:

1. Start either the OS/2 System Editor (in the Productivity folder) or the IBM Works Editor (in the IBM Works folder).

Two Ways to Go   To start the IBM Works editor, you can double-click on the IBM Works icon and select Word Processor from the dialog box or you can drag a Document template into a folder and double-click on it.

2. If you want to edit an existing file, open it now. (For help, see Lesson 17.)

3. Click the mouse pointer where you want to begin, and start typing. When the words reach the right margin, they are automatically bumped down to the next line. For this reason, do not press Enter at the end of every line. Only press Enter to start a new paragraph (Figure 22.1).

4. After you enter and make changes to your text, be sure to save your file. See Lesson 17 for help.

The Exception: OS/2 System Editor
When you use the System Editor, you *do* have to press Enter to go to the next line, as you would

with a typewriter. However, you can turn on Word wrap if you want to make the OS/2 System Editor act like all other word processors and editors. To do that, open the Options menu, select Word wrap, and then select On.

Press Enter to add a blank line.

Press Enter to end a paragraph.

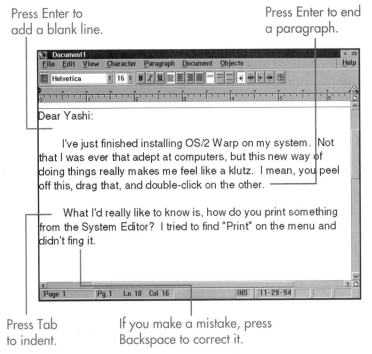

Press Tab to indent.

If you make a mistake, press Backspace to correct it.

Figure 22.1 Entering text is simple.

Follow these additional instructions when entering text:

- If you make a mistake, press Backspace to erase it or select the text and press Delete.

- To indent a paragraph, press Tab. Do not use the Spacebar to do anything except insert a space between words or sentences.

- Normally, when you type text, it is inserted at the cursor position and any existing text is moved over to make room for the new text. If you want to type over existing text, press Insert once. That turns on

Overtype mode, in which whatever text you type replaces whatever's already there. Press Insert again to return to regular (Insert) mode.

Moving Around the Document

As you type, the cursor advances to follow you. But if you want to change a word in the previous paragraph, do you have to backspace and erase what you typed, and then type it over? No, you don't. You can move the cursor to a particular location by simply clicking on that location. For example, to insert something before a particular word, click in front of that word and start typing.

You can also move the cursor with the arrow keys on your keyboard if you want. To move to the beginning of a line (left margin), press Home. To move to the end of a line (right margin), press End. To move to the beginning or end of the file, press Ctrl+Home or Ctrl+End. If you have a long document, you can scroll to where you want by clicking on the scroll arrows.

Selecting Text

To make changes to your text, you must first select it. You can then copy, move, delete, or format the selected text. To select text with the mouse, follow these steps:

1. Click the left mouse button at the beginning of the text you want to select.

2. Continue to hold down the mouse button, and drag over the text you want to select. Your text appears *highlighted*, as shown in Figure 22.2.

If you select the wrong text, just click anywhere in the document, and the highlighted text returns to normal.

Selected text

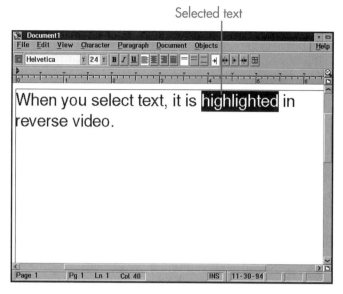

Figure 22.2 When you select text, it's displayed in reverse video.

Copying, Moving, and Deleting Text

After you select your text, you can copy, move, or delete it. When you copy text, you place an exact duplicate somewhere else in the file and the original remains intact. Follow these steps to copy text:

1. Select the text you want to copy.

2. Open the Edit menu and select Copy (or press Ctrl+Insert).

3. Click on the location in the document to which you want to copy the text.

4. Open the Edit menu and select Paste (or press Shift+Insert).

I Didn't Mean to Do That   If you move, copy, or delete something accidentally, you can use the Undo command to get it back—if you act *immediately*. Open the Edit menu and select Undo to undo the last change. (You can only undo the very last change you made.)

When you move text, you actually remove the text from its original position and place it somewhere else. Follow these steps to move text:

1. Select the text you want to move.

2. Open the Edit menu and select Cut (or press Shift+Delete).

3. Click on the location in the document to which you want to move the text.

4. Open the Edit menu and select Paste (or press Shift+Insert).

If you simply want to delete text, follow these steps:

1. Select the text you want to delete.

2. Press Delete.

Formatting Text

You can add formatting (bold, italic, underline, unusual fonts, and so on) to your document with the IBM Works editor.

What About the Other Editors?   The OS/2 System Editor cannot handle document formatting; use it to edit simple text files, such as the AUTOEXEC.BAT and the CONFIG.SYS. Although the Enhanced Editor can handle formatting, it's very difficult to use. Your best bet is to use IBM Works.

To add formatting to a document using IBM Works:

1. Select the text you want to format.

2. Click on the appropriate button on the Ribbon (see Figure 22.3).

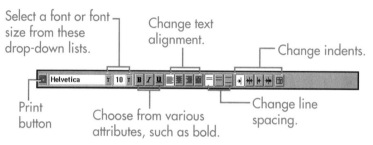

Figure 22.3 Formatting with the Ribbon.

Printing Your Document

Using IBM Works, you print your document the same way you would print any other Works file.

1. Right-click on the Print button (it's on the Ribbon in front of the font drop-down list box).

2. Drag the Print button icon to the Printer object and release the mouse button.

To print a file created with the OS/2 System Editor, save the file and exit the program. Then drag the data-file object to the Printer object.

In this lesson, you learned how to use the editors that come with OS/2 to edit letters, memos, and simple files such as AUTOEXEC.BAT. In the next lesson, you'll learn how to use the spreadsheet and chart programs in IBM Works.

Lesson

Number Crunching

In this lesson, you'll learn how to use the Spreadsheet and Chart programs included in IBM Works.

Spreadsheet Basics

A spreadsheet is made up of rows and columns. Rows run horizontally and are numbered along the left-hand side of the sheet: 1, 2, 3, and so on. Columns run vertically and are labeled along the top of the sheet: A to Z, then AA, AB, and so on.

Where a particular row and a column intersect, they form a *cell*. You enter your data (*labels* and *values*) into these cells. Labels provide a title or description for a particular column or row, while values (numbers and formulas) provide the data to be calculated.

Cells are identified according to where they're located in the spreadsheet. For example, cell A3 is located where column A intersects row 3 (see Figure 23.1).

Starting the Spreadsheet Program

You can start the spreadsheet program in one of two ways:

- By double-clicking on the IBM Works icon and selecting Spreadsheet.

    or

- By dragging a Sheet template into a folder and double-clicking on it.

Column A   Cell A3

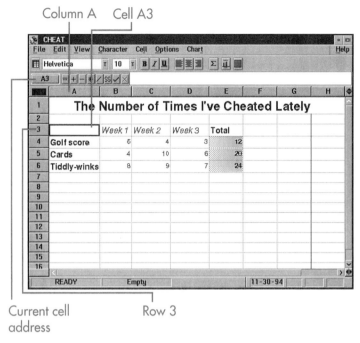

Current cell
address

Row 3

Figure 23.1   A spreadsheet is made up of rows and columns.

Entering Numbers and Labels

Before you start entering data, take a moment to think about how the spreadsheet should look. What do you want to track?

Down column A, list the things you want to track (such as names, department numbers, or in this case, games). Across row 1, list either units of measure (such as dollars, percentages, or sales units) or time (such as months, quarters, or years). In my example, I tracked games in which I've cheated and used weeks as my unit of measure.

To enter numbers or text into a cell, follow these steps:

1. Move the cursor to the cell in which you want to enter data. To move the cursor, click in the cell you

want or navigate there using the arrow keys. The
current cell is highlighted, as shown in Figure 23.2.

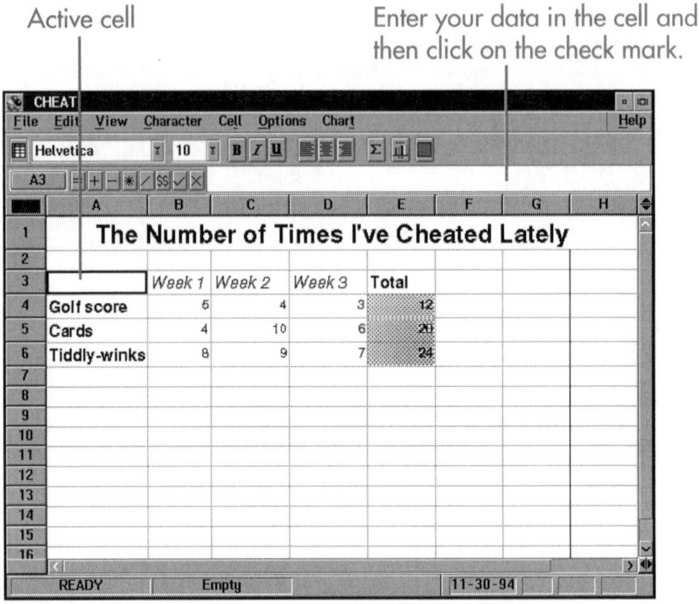

Active cell   Enter your data in the cell and
                                     then click on the check mark.

Figure 23.2 Entering data into the spreadsheet.

2. Enter a label, a value, or a formula (you'll learn how
   to enter formulas later in this lesson). What you
   type appears in the cell edit box.

3. Press Enter or click on the check mark button to
   confirm your entry. It then appears in the selected
   cell. (If you make a mistake before you press Enter,
   you can click on the X button to undo your entry. If
   you make a mistake *after* entering something, just
   click on the cell again and retype your entry.)

Formatting Your Spreadsheet

As you're entering data, you can format it (change the way it looks). For example, to change the font, attributes, or shading of selected cells, click on the appropriate button on the Ribbon, as shown in Figure 23.3.

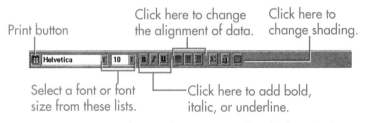

Click here to change the alignment of data.

Click here to change shading.

Print button

Select a font or font size from these lists.

Click here to add bold, italic, or underline.

Figure 23.3   Change the way your data looks with the Ribbon.

If you want to change the way numbers look, experiment with the Number commands on the Cell menu. If a column isn't wide enough to display its data, you'll see ####### or scientific notation. To change the width of a column, click on its right edge and drag.

Creating Formulas

With formulas, you can add, subtract, multiply, and divide (in short, do all those things you need to do with numbers). All formulas begin with an equal sign (=). The equal sign tells IBM Works that you're entering a formula instead of a simple value or label. In a formula, you use a plus sign (+) for addition, a minus sign (–) for subtraction, an asterisk (*) for multiplication, and a slash (/) for division.

Here's how to enter a formula:

1. Click in the cell in which you want the result of the formula to appear.

2. Type =.

3. Type a cell address or a number.

4. Type the operator (+, −, *, or /).

5. Type another cell address or a number.

6. Repeat steps 4 and 5 as needed. When you're done entering the formula, press Enter or click on the check mark button.

> **Mouse Shortcut** If you don't feel like typing, you can click on the =, +, −, *, and / buttons to the left of the cell edit box and click on the cells you want to include in the formula.

For example, to add a total to the row of golf scores in the example spreadsheet shown in Figure 23.2, I entered =B4+C4+D4 into cell E4. Notice that there aren't any spaces in the formula.

> **Quick Sum** The Sum function makes total formulas easier to enter. Instead of typing the address of every cell you want to add, just click in the cell in which you want the total displayed and click on the Sum button (it looks like the Greek letter sigma). Drag the cursor over the cells you want to add and press Enter. Your formula will look something like =SUM(B5:D5), which is the same as =B5+C5+D5.

Copying Formulas

When you copy a formula, it is adjusted automatically to fit the row or column you copy it to. For example, in the spreadsheet in Figure 23.2, cell E4 contains the formula =SUM(B4:D4). When I copied that formula to cell E5, the formula was automatically adjusted to fit its new row: =SUM(B5:D5).

To copy a formula, follow these steps:

1. Click in the cell that contains the formula you want to copy.

2. Open the Edit menu and select Copy (or press Ctrl+Insert).

3. Select the cell or cells to which you want to copy the formula.

4. Open the Edit menu and select Paste (or press Shift+Insert).

Printing Your Spreadsheet

You print your spreadsheet the same way you print any file from within an IBM Works program.

1. Right-click on the Print button (it's on the Ribbon in front of the font drop-down list box).

2. Drag the Print button icon to the Printer object and release the mouse button.

Creating a Chart

Although you can start the Chart program and enter your chart data separately, the easiest way to create a chart is through the Spreadsheet program. The following steps walk you through this method of creating a chart:

1. Enter the numbers you want to chart into the spreadsheet program and select them.

2. Click on the Chart button on the Ribbon. The cursor changes to a small cross.

3. Click in the spreadsheet to establish the upper left-hand corner of the chart. Drag downward and to the right to mark an area for the chart if you want to

size the area for the chart. When you release the
mouse button, the chart appears, formatted as a bar
chart.

4. To make changes to the chart, double-click on it,
   and the Chart program starts.

Choosing a Chart Type

By default, your data is graphed on a bar chart. However, you
can select another chart type by clicking on the appropriate
button on the Ribbon. In addition, you can give each chart a
3-D effect by clicking on the 3-D button on the Ribbon (see
Figure 23.4).

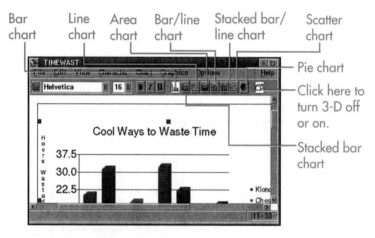

Figure 23.4 Use the Ribbon to change chart types.

These guidelines will help you distinguish the various
chart types and determine which one you might want to use:

Use a bar or stacked bar chart to compare individual units, such as the value of each stock in your
portfolio. These charts are also great for illustrating
changes over time, such as the increase in lines on
your face since you learned OS/2.

Use a pie chart to compare the relationships between the parts of a whole, such as the revenue from
five different products.

Use a line chart to illustrate changes over time, such
as the rise in medical costs or the decline in loose
change in your pocket.

Use an area chart to emphasize change, like the
change in your mood now that some of this is starting
to make sense.

Use a scatter chart to determine whether there's a
correlation between one set of data and another.

Understanding the Parts of a Chart

There are many parts to a chart, all of which you can change
through commands you'll find on the Options menu. Figure
23.5 shows the parts of a typical chart.

The purpose of the title is easy to figure out, but some
of the other chart parts may not be so obvious:

X-axis and Y-axis titles   These optional titles act as
labels for the values plotted along each axis.

Data series   A particular range of values within a
chart. For example, the sales revenue for a single
salesperson could represent a series.

Legend   This provides the description for the separate data series in a chart. You'll find a legend in every
pie chart, but you might also find them in charts when
there is more than one data series (see Figure 23.5).

One color equals one
series on this chart.   Title   Legend

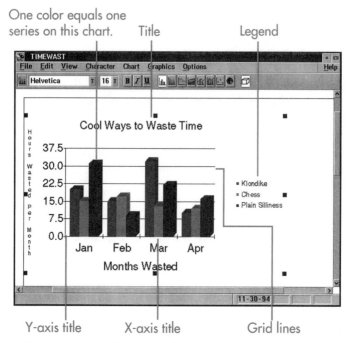

Y-axis title   X-axis title   Grid lines

Figure 23.5 The parts of a chart.

Grid lines Lines that help you read your chart and
determine what's what. You'll find this option hidden
under Axes.

In this lesson, you learned how to use the Spreadsheet
and Chart programs included with IBM Works. In the next
lesson, you'll learn how to customize OS/2.

Lesson

Customizing OS/2

In this lesson, you'll learn how to customize the OS/2 environment.

Colorizing OS/2

If you want to add more color to OS/2, you can. You can change the color of just about anything, including the Desktop, the interior of a window, a window's title bar, the text under an object, the buttons on the LaunchPad, and the LaunchPad itself. Here's how:

1. Open the OS/2 System folder.

2. Open the System Setup folder.

3. Double-click on the Solid Color Palette icon. If you want a wider choice of colors, double-click on the Mixed Color Palette instead.

4. Right-click on a color and drag it inside a window, onto a title bar, or onto the Desktop, and then release the mouse button. The object becomes that color (see Figure 24.1).

To change the color of text, press and hold the Ctrl key as you drag a color on top of the text. To change all the windows or all the title bars to the same color in one step, press and hold the Alt key as you drag. To change the color of the text in all windows or all title bars, press and hold Alt+Ctrl as you drag.

You can color the Desktop.

You can change the color of text.

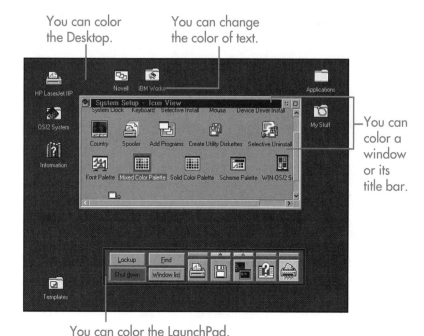

You can color a window or its title bar.

You can color the LaunchPad.

Figure 24.1 OS/2 in color.

Using the Scheme Palette

By selecting an overall color scheme, you can change the color of all windows, all title bars, and the Desktop in one simple step with the Scheme Palette. Follow these steps:

1. Open the OS/2 System folder.

2. Open the System Setup folder.

3. Double-click on the Scheme Palette icon.

4. Right-click on a scheme, drag it onto the Desktop, and release the mouse button. The Desktop, windows, title bars, and so on change to fit the scheme.

Changing the Background with a Bitmap

Instead of changing the color of the Desktop or a window, you can add a *bitmap*. The following steps show you how.

> **Bitmap**   A computerized picture made up of tiny dots, like the millions of dots that fill your TV screen.

1. Right-click on the Desktop (or any other window whose background you want to change) and select Settings.

2. Click on the Background tab.

3. Select a bitmap (picture) from the drop-down list. The Preview area lets you view your selection.

4. Double-click on the title-bar icon. The bitmap fills the background of the Desktop or the window you selected, as shown in Figure 24.2.

You can add a bitmap to the Desktop or the background of a window.

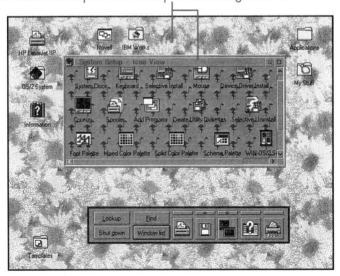

Figure 24.2   Use a bitmap as a background.

Can't Windows Do This?   Yes, in
Windows you can choose from an equally
long list of backgrounds that they call
"wallpaper." However, only OS/2 lets you
change the background of every window, not just the
Desktop.

Changing the Screen Resolution

If your monitor is a Super VGA (instead of a standard VGA-
type), you can change the resolution at which you view
OS/2. If you have a Super VGA monitor, OS/2 has already set
you up with various types of resolutions. All you have to do
is change to a higher resolution to see a sharper image on-
screen. However, there is one drawback: the higher the
resolution, the smaller your objects appear. (With such a fine
screen, things can be smaller and still look sharp.) This also
means that you'll be able to drag more objects onto your
Desktop without feeling like you're elbow-to-elbow.

Resolution   The resolution, such as 640 ×
480 or 1024 × 768, refers to the number of
pixels on your screen. A pixel is a dot, and these
dots make up the image you see on-screen. The
more pixels there are, the better your screen looks.

Follow these steps to change the screen resolution:

1. Open the System Setup folder.

2. Double-click on the System object.

3. Click on the Screen tab, and then under Screen
resolution, select the video mode you want to use.

4. Close the notebook and restart your PC.

What If Something Goes Wrong? If
something goes wrong after you change resolutions, just reboot and press Alt+F1 when you see
the tiny white box that appears in the upper left-
hand corner of the screen. Eventually you'll see a list of
Recovery choices. Press V to restore the previous version
of the Desktop.

If you don't see the right resolutions listed when you try
the System object, you might have to install the extra device
drivers (special programs that help OS/2 control the monitor) that came with your monitor. Follow these steps:

1. Open the OS/2 System folder.

2. Open the System Setup folder.

3. Double-click on the Device Driver Install icon.

4. Insert the device driver diskette that came with
   your monitor. Change the source drive to that same
   diskette drive, and then click on Install.

Changing the Size of Icons

You can shrink the size of the OS/2 icons so you can fit more
of them on your screen, as shown in Figure 24.3. If, on the
other hand, you have a high resolution monitor and you find
the icons too small, you can enlarge them.

Follow these steps to change the size of your icons:

1. Right-click on the Desktop and select Settings.

2. Click on the View tab.

3. Under Icon display, click on whatever you want:
   Normal size or Small size. You can see how it will
   look if you drag the box out of your way so you can
   view the Desktop.

4. Double-click on the title-bar icon to close the
   notebook.

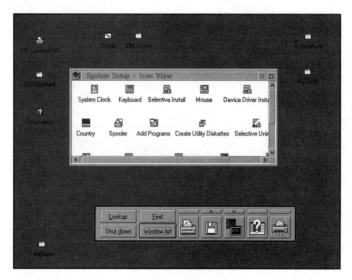

Figure 24.3 You can change the size of icons.

There is one disadvantage to shrinking the size of the icons: if you like the size of the icons, you have to repeat these steps within every folder (window). The Desktop settings only change the icons on the Desktop.

In this lesson, you learned how to customize OS/2 Warp in various ways. In the next lesson, you'll learn how to install new programs and devices under Warp.

Lesson

Installing New Programs and Devices

In this lesson, you'll learn how to install new programs and devices under OS/2 Warp.

Creating the Start Button for a New Program

Installing a new program is a two-part process. First, you run the application's install or setup program, which basically copies the program's files onto your PC's hard disk. When that's done, you're ready for part two, which involves creating the program's "start button" (icon).

> **This Isn't How I Did It in Windows**
> When you install a program in Windows, Windows usually creates the start button icon for you; but when you install a DOS program, you're on your own. To make things consistent, OS/2 has you go through the same steps every time you add a new program, whether it's a Windows, OS/2, or DOS program.

Follow these steps to create a start button for a program you've just installed or to replace a start button you've deleted accidentally:

1. Open the OS/2 System folder. Open the System Setup folder.

2. Double-click on the Add Programs object.

3. Click on Search for and select programs to add, and then click on OK.

4. Select the option (OS/2, Windows, or DOS) that corresponds with your new program by clicking on the other options to deselect them. (If you're adding a new Windows program, be sure to select both Windows programs and Windows Groups.)

5. To start the scan process, click on OK.

6. When the search process is complete, Select Programs produces a list of programs. Select what you want to add and click on OK. OS/2 creates icons for the programs you select and places them in a convenient folder. Windows programs are usually found in the WIN-OS/2 Groups folder; OS/2 programs are found in the OS/2 Programs folder; DOS programs are placed in the DOS Programs folder.

> **I Don't See My Program**   If your program doesn't appear on the Select Programs list, click on the Other Programs button. Under Program Type, click on the type of program you're looking for. Then scroll down the Available Programs list until you find your program; click on it. Then click on Add and click on OK.

Changing the Settings of a DOS Program

DOS programs can be very demanding, yelling and screaming for immediate access to the printer, the monitor, or the mouse. When they don't get what they want when they want it, they can blow up in your face, act real strange, or ignore you completely. If that happens to one of your DOS programs, try changing one or two of its settings at a time (as described here) until the problem is fixed.

1. Right-click on the DOS program's icon and select Settings.

2. Click on the Session tab.

3. Click on DOS Settings.

4. Select All Dos settings and click on OK. The DOS Settings dialog box appears.

5. Change only the settings you *have* to (see Table 25.1 for help). Then click on OK. Your changes take place immediately.

6. To leave the notebook, double-click on the title-bar icon.

I Made a Mistake!   If you make a mistake, just go back to the Settings notebook and click on the Default button on the page where you changed something.

Test It   You can test some of these settings while your program is running so you can change them before you make a permanent commitment. Start your DOS program in a window (or press Alt + Home), click once on the title-bar icon, and select DOS Settings. Change your setting as usual. Of course there's a price for all this convenience: the settings you change are for *this time only*. To make them permanent, change them as described in the numbered steps.

Table 25.1 The Most Likely DOS Settings to Change

Setting	What to Do with It
COM_DIRECT_ACCESS	For a communications program, set to ON.
COM_HOLD	For a communications program, set to ON.
DOS_BACKGROUND_EXECUTION	You might want to change this to OFF for game programs.
DOS_DEVICE	Use this to load a device driver for one special program. (To load for all DOS programs, put the command in the CONFIG.SYS.)
DOS_HIGH	Gives a game program a larger room to play in.
EMS_MEMORY_LIMIT	Gives your program expanded memory. Check the manual for the amount, but try at least 2048.
HW_ROM_TO_RAM	Makes your DOS program faster by moving hardware instructions into memory. For a communications or game program, set to ON.
IDLE_SECONDS	Sets the amount of time a program can sit and do nothing before OS/2 moves on to something else. For a communications or game program, set to 60.

Setting	What to Do with It
IDLE_SENSITIVITY	You can slow down a DOS program by setting this lower than 75. For a communications or game program, set higher than 75.
INT_DURING_IO	Stops programs from writing to disk when your communications program is in the middle of receiving a file. Benefits intense games.
MOUSE_EXCLUSIVE_ACCESS	If you're seeing double (mouse pointers, that is), set this to ON.
VIDEO_FASTPASTE	Set to ON to speed up copying and pasting between DOS programs and OS/2 or Windows. Good for slow games, but may freak some programs.
VIDEO_ONDEMAND_	Turn to OFF if you're having MEMORY trouble with high-tech games.
VIDEO_ROM_EMULATION	Some games like this; others don't.
VIDEO_RETRACE_EMULATION	Set to OFF if you want to run a game in a full screen.
VIDEO_WINDOW_REFRESH	If your DOS program acts jerky on-screen, increase this number.

Installing a Printer, CD-ROM, Sound Card, Mouse, or SCSI Device

If you've recently bought a new device (such as a CD-ROM, tape backup, sound card, or joystick) for your PC, there are a few steps you must complete before OS/2 can use them.

1. First, connect your new device to your PC. Then install the *device driver*.

> **Device Driver**   Special program that acts as a "translator" between the PC and some optional device, such as a printer, CD-ROM, or tape backup.

2. To install the device driver, open the OS/2 System folder, open the System Setup folder, and double-click on the Selective Install icon. The System Configuration box appears.

3. Click on the button for the device you want to install. (For example, to install a CD-ROM, click on the CD-ROM button.)

4. Select your specific brand name from the list that appears. (For example, select NEC MultiSpin 4Xe.)

5. Click on OK.

6. Select OK to use the default settings for the device or click on Selections to change them.

7. Click on Install and click OK. Then insert whatever diskettes it asks for. Your new object appears on the Desktop when you're through.

How Do I Install My Modem?   In Windows you install the modem once and programs that use the modem ask Windows what to do. With OS/2, you install the support for your modem through your communications program, such as HyperAccess Lite or OS2-CIM. See that program's Help system for more information.

Installing Other Devices

If you need to install something you don't see listed in the System Configuration box (a joystick, a network card, or a video card, for example), follow these steps to install the device driver (you'll need the device driver diskette that came with your new device):

1. Open the OS/2 System folder, open the System Setup folder, and double-click on the Device Drive Install icon.

2. Insert your device driver diskette.

3. Under Destination directory, type the location to which you want OS/2 to copy the device files.

4. Click on Install and follow the directions on-screen.

In this lesson, you learned how to install programs and devices under OS/2 Warp. This is the last lesson.

Index

subdirectories, 65
Super VGA monitors, 164-165
switching, 41, 99-100
System Editor, 145-150

T

Telnet sites, 140-141
templates, 10, 97
    creating, 111-112
    data-files, changing into
        templates, 49
    folders, creating new, 64-66
    objects, copying, 60
Templates folder, 10
text
    copying/moving, 149-150
    formatting, 150-151
    searching for, 70-71
    selecting, 148-149
text boxes, dialog boxes, 46
text editors, 145-151
    Enhanced Editor, 145
    IBM Works, 145-152
    System Editor, 145-150
Tile command (Desktop menu), 37
title bar, colorizing, 161-162
Tree view, 39, 86
Tutorial (Help system), 9-10, 25-27

U

Ultimedia Lite/2 folder, 136-137
UNDELETE command, 129
UNDELETE program, 81-83
Undo command (Edit menu), 38, 150
URLs (universal resource locators),
    World Wide Web, 143
USENET, 139-140
utilities, Internet, 135-144

V

values (spreadsheets), 152
Veronica, Gopher, 138
video cards, installing, 173
views
    Detail view, 86
    drive windows, 86-88
    Tree view, 86
    windows, changing, 39-41

W-Z

WebExplorer, 141-144
wild cards, 24, 70
Window list, 14, 32
window menus, 43
Windows
    program groups, 6
    programs
        printing, 114
        running, 126
        starting, 89
        switching, 123
    running, 123-126
    sharing data, 116-117
windows
    arranging, 37-39
    bitmap backgrounds, 163-164
    cascading, 37-38
    closing, 29
    colors, changing, 50
    Drive A window, 76
    Drive C windows, 76
    drives windows, 86-88
    maximizing, 32-34
    minimizing, 31-32
    moving, 30
    objects, arranging, 38-39
    opening, 29
    resizing, 33-34
    scroll bars, 35
    switching, 41
    tiling, 37-38
    title bar, colorizing, 161-162
    views, 39-41
    window menus, 43
    Windows, running within,
        124-126
Windows Programs, starting, 98
World Wide Web, 141-144